MERCY
for
ME

*The True Story of a Couple on a Journey
through the Valley of the Shadow of Death*

ARLIE RAUCH

WESTBOW®
PRESS
A DIVISION OF THOMAS NELSON
& ZONDERVAN

Scripture taken from the NEW AMERICAN STANDARD
BIBLE, © 1960, 1962, 1963, 1968, 1971, 1972, 1973, 1975,
1977, by the Lockman Foundation. Used by permission.

WestBow Press books may be ordered through booksellers or by contacting:

WestBow Press
A Division of Thomas Nelson
1663 Liberty Drive
Bloomington, IN 47403
www.westbowpress.com
1 (866) 928-1240

ISBN: 978-1-4908-2210-5 (sc)
ISBN: 978-1-4908-2209-9 (e)

Library of Congress Control Number: 2014900400

Printed in the United States of America.

WestBow Press rev. date: 01/15/2014

To Ruth who in the providence of God is still
my companion for the journey of this life,
whose courage is remarkable, and whose music
I love to hear as I work in the office.

CONTENTS

PROLOGUE

December 19, 2011, was my sixty-fourth birthday.

In the morning Ruth and I drove twenty-eight miles east to Wibaux, MT, to enjoy coffee at the new Testarossa. It was a small coffee shop, and, as was usual, we engaged in conversation with some local people who happened in while we were there.

Back in Glendive, about 1:30 in the afternoon, Ruth joined several other ladies for a weekly prayer time to pray for people with various kinds of needs. Because the weather was unseasonably mild I went for a ride on my motorcycle. At 3:30 Ruth and I met in my basement office to read emails that had just arrived. While we were doing this Ruth complained of a severe headache suddenly making itself known. (Headaches were not a common occurrence for her.) I suggested she go upstairs and take something for it. She delayed and a few minutes later said she was becoming queasy, so she went to our bedroom on the main floor to lie down.

Later I went up and asked her if she needed anything. She said she was cool, so I got a small blanket—her favorite, one she had made—and put it over her. She apologized for not being able to join me to make supper together as we had planned. We were going to make my old favorite, cheese pockets, like my mother used to make. She told me there was corn chowder in the refrigerator that I could warm up.

I put the the corn chowder on the stove and turned the burner on low. I decided to watch the evening news while the chowder heated.

I heard Ruth get up and go to the bathroom. A bit later I heard a noise like something had struck the plastic waste basket beside the toilet. I walked toward the bathroom, called her name, and heard no answer. I entered and found her crumpled on the floor between the toilet and the tub. When she fell, her legs had folded underneath her. So I straightened her out on her back. There was no life in her eyes. She was breathing erratically and noisily.

Two thoughts immediately made themselves known: our only hope is in God, and I must call 911.

Our life changed in an instant. We were unplugged from life as we knew it. And so began the strangest period of our life.

ACKNOWLEDGMENTS

Many thanks go to Patti Nefzger who invested much time in carefully editing the book. Her influence appears on virtually every page. Her expertise was significant throughout as she fixed mistakes and clarified what might otherwise have been misunderstood.

Thanks go also to all those named in the book. Each of them was a participant in this journey.

I want to thank those who encouraged me to write. Their suggestions pushed me and sustained me to record what happened so that family and friends could know the whole story. Included here must be our family. They were supportive throughout the journey, showed interest my writing, and even provided quotations that could be used in the book.

Thanks to Westbow Press for their services to make this available to the public.

Finally, I want to thank our Lord and Savior Jesus Christ, the Giver of life, Who made Himself known to us in special ways; He was with us all the way. To Him be the glory!

As I walked into Mom's critical care room in Denver to see her for the first time, her eyes and lips went into communication-less motion. I was told she recognized me. This was the only time I saw her alert for many days.

The Holy Spirit, the Spirit of Truth and Comforter, massively supported me (John 15:26; 14:26). When the "bottom" dropped out, I sank into God's rising comfort. The Holy Spirit impressed upon me that He would never leave Mom and would continually and perfectly minister to her soul, mind, and body as only He could do. She would not be without the triune God— ever —on earth or in heaven. Just a day or two later, Dad shared Romans 8:26. We didn't have to know what to pray because the Holy Spirit was interceding for us!

The Holy Spirit used these truths and the truths of our secure salvation and His loving sovereignty to comfort me over and over.

Merrily and Hans

None of us knows what tomorrow, today no less, will bring. On December 19, Monica and I received word that Mom was on her way to the hospital in an ambulance. There was great sadness that day and uncertainty in the outcome, but what a blessing to be able to seek the Lord in His ability to heal and His willingness to bear our burdens and seek comfort in His faithfulness, sovereignty and loving-kindness. While we do not know why the Lord allowed this to happen, good times are not necessarily the best for our souls. Praise the Lord for restoring Mom and for strengthening Dad through it all. Praise the Lord for the demonstration of love by so many during this time.

Andrae and Monica

Peace. It is a fruit of the children of God, those who are sealed in the Spirit (Gal. 5:22-23). It is promised to us as a result of laying ourselves and our deepest desires before God in prayer when our natural bent is to be anxious (Phil. 4:6-7). Knowing that our hearts would be prone to fear and feeling troubled, a peace, not of this world, was bequeathed to us by Jesus (John 14:27).

We remember getting the first news from Dad, a succinct email he sent out as Mom was en route to the hospital. That same morning there was the first skype call from Merrily, followed by much waiting as the operation, the first critical hours, and the "not out of the woods yet" days unfolded. All these firsts turned our life upside down. We didn't know if we would see Mom alive again and we were halfway across the world from the situation. Our minds were consumed with wondering and projecting and waiting to hear. But this difficulty that wrapped itself around our hearts and minds also drove us to prayer. As I did the dishes, prayed with Sy, and tried to keep going in life, I surrendered my mom, my wishes for her, and her future to my heavenly Father. And as difficult as this whole experience was we knew His peace. In crying out to Him He was faithful and met us with "the peace…what surpasses comprehension and is able to guard your hearts and your minds in Christ Jesus."

Peace manifested itself in different ways. We rested in the fact that our siblings were caring for Dad and Mom. We saw God's hand of provision and faithfulness in the details. We felt 100% okay with waiting at home (far away from America, Denver, and Montana) until the time that Mom would return home and I could then lend a helping hand.

As this is being written the year anniversary of Mom's aneurism is rapidly approaching. We praise the Lord for what has transpired in her life in the past year. Of course, we think of Mom's miraculous recovery, but, with overflowing gratitude, we can't forget walking with the Lord in His peace when the days were darkest. Thank you, Lord, for your goodness to our family.

Renessa and Sy

Hearing the news that our mother was seriously ill was almost unreal. Being far away, there was nothing we could do to visit or help right away. We turned to God to pray for healing for Mom, with the understanding that God could say "no" and take her home to be with Him. We gave thanks that Mom was a believer and knew that death held nothing bad for her. We were more concerned for Dad and what he was going through. Again, we trusted God to provide Dad strength and comfort and knew that there were many in Glendive who were able to support Dad in person and many more around the world that were lifting Dad up in spirit.

Our time in Denver with Dad and Mom was very special. We were blessed to be present when Mom was coming back to being herself. Being with Dad was amazing, to see a man of God go through such a trying time. He was a man who dearly loved his wife, had almost lost her, and was now overjoyed at the prospect of having her back. He didn't know what the future held, but he trusted God to provide and knew he would do whatever was required of him to care for his love. I have always enjoyed Dad's teaching, but it was extra special to hear him speak of encouragement from the Scriptures in light of his current suffering.

The first time we saw Mom, she was just waking up and didn't recognize us. The next time, there was a spark of understanding. In the week we were with Dad and Mom, we saw Mom go from just lying in bed and making eye contact to being able to sit up and whisper. I really enjoyed talking with Mom, telling her stories of everything that was happening at home with our little girl, with our home, with Christy. We had our laptop along and found pictures and videos of Ella and Mom watched them intently. In this time, I was especially thankful for Christy. She is a registered nurse and was key in motivating Mom in her rehab and getting her started on her road to therapy and recovery.

Carmody and Christy

INTRODUCTION

Ruth and I met while studying at Grace Bible Institute (now Grace University) in Omaha, Nebraska. In June of 1971 we were married near Ruth's hometown of Beatrice, Nebraska.

For Ruth, early married life consisted of two years teaching third grade in public school. Then came four children in less than ten years—girl, boy, girl, boy. Her life as a wife and mother was full, and yet during all that time she also taught piano students.

Early married life for me involved studies in university and seminary. In 1974 I entered pastoral ministry and have been a pastor ever since. I served churches in South Dakota, Nebraska, and Montana. Since 1990 Ruth and I have served the Community Bible Church of Glendive, Montana. In 1977 I also began servicing pianos as a part-time business and have continued that more or less since.

Most couples in church ministry are involved in numerous ways in the lives of others, and this has certainly been the case for us. Ruth has been involved in church life musically, playing piano and organ, as well as in children's and women's ministries. She has also been involved outside the church in community and school music events (as accompanist, teacher, and adjudicator). She has been active in a food coop because she is interested in nutrition as well as thrift. She also has been committed to distance walking and other forms of exercise.

I have been involved in church ministries of preaching/teaching, Sunday school, AWANA youth ministry, counseling, and also music. Outside our church I have been involved in the local ministerial association and, for a time, Toastmasters. I have also produced a Christian radio program for over twenty years. Together Ruth and I have provided services from time to time at a nursing home and at a fourth-offense DUI facility.

Our hobbies, including gardening, bee-keeping, chess and motorcycling, existed for relaxation and also as provision for the family. Life has not been dull.

By the year 2000 all the children had graduated from high school, and by 2003 they had graduated from college at least once. Today all four are married, and there are currently eight grandchildren. They live in Minnesota, California, Arizona, and Central Asia. We do not see them frequently.

Ruth and I have become accustomed to living as just the two of us at home; we deeply love each other, and it has been our goal from the beginning to live out the picture of the relationship of Christ to His Church outlined in

Ephesians 5. My office is at home, and this has allowed us to be together much. We have enjoyed our time spent together at home and on special vacations when we have been able to participate in adventures significant to both of us.

All of this came to a screeching halt that December day when I found Ruth crumpled on the floor. Who knew what had happened and what would happen? Who could say when—or if—life would ever return to normal? Only God knew, and this is the story of His involvement with us since that day.

I am as surprised as anyone that I am writing this kind of book. A theological work would have been more likely, or an exegetical book explaining some passage of Scripture. I have been a careful student of the Scriptures since before entering the pastorate.

The Bible should be not only the source of what we believe, but also the source for how we live. For example, we sincerely sought to incorporate the wisdom of Proverbs in our marriage and in our family life. We can vouch for the fact that God's wisdom is practical.

But as we grappled with this experience, numerous people suggested that I should write a book about our journey. I had shared with hundreds of people through a Care Page on the internet. Many said they were blessed by it, though my goal at that time was less grandiose. I simply wrote what

I was thinking day by day as Ruth teetered on the edge of life and death and then as she began to wake and begin the long road of therapy and recovery.

Because of my immersion in the Scriptures my thoughts naturally went to the Bible. But in addition, the many issues I faced stripped away everything superfluous, and the little, taken-for-granted items of life became significant. These I shared as we became very sensitive to them.

I didn't write down everything that happened or every thought I had on the Care Page. I did keep a daily journal during that time; I called it simply "Sequence." There were email exchanges with a variety of people, especially at the beginning. And then, there was knowledge and meditation to which I alone was privy.

Even though effort was made to write accurately, some facts, especially dates, may be questionable. Careful attention to the above sources, in addition to interviews with involved people, should have corrected most of these issues. In any case I take responsibility for any errors in the book.

This book contains drama, drama we never expected and surely never requested. But it contains more than that, and that "more" is what I really wish to communicate. It is the story of God walking with two insignificant people through the valley of the shadow of death. It is the story of God choreographing recovery from trauma that is amazing, if not miraculous. It is the story of Jesus showing that in the end, what truly matters is a relationship with Him. It is the story of an experience in which one man's insides were painfully wrenched, and at the same time filled to overflowing with God's guidance, love, goodness, and mercy.

Much has been said and written elsewhere about the stress of being the caregiver of someone passing through such an illness. I do not write as a caregiver—I write as a husband.

If this book can move you in the direction of trusting God as He is revealed to us in the Bible, then it will have been worth every effort.

It is possible to read the narrative of what happened by reading in sequence only the chapters beginning with "Stage…." The "Other Side" chapters record my processing of events.

CHAPTER 1

STAGE ONE—FROM GLENDIVE TO DENVER

I quickly called 911 (around 5:30 PM), and within a couple minutes two police officers who had been in the neighborhood were at the door. One of them was also an EMT. Their sergeant arrived shortly after the officers and said the ambulance was on the way.

Soon the ambulance arrived. Since the bathroom did not have much floor space, they could not transfer Ruth to a stretcher there, so they carried her out by means of a mega mover sheet. I told them I would drive myself to the hospital, and they were off.

Before leaving the house I sent an email to the children and to our church's prayer chain. It read:

> Ruth had a strong headache a couple hours
> ago. Then nausea. She went to bed. She
> went to the bathroom. I heard a noise.
> She had crumpled up, fallen. She is in the
> hospital unconscious. I'm going there now.
> Please pray for us.

It seemed important to me that all of them know of the emergency, though at that time no one really understood what had happened.

At the hospital a CT scan and other tests, which produced a diagnosis of a stroke, resulted in the decision to send Ruth on to Billings, MT, the closest city with specialized healthcare.

The wait for the plane from Billings Clinic seemed longer than necessary. Later I learned that both of their planes had been unavailable, but they borrowed a plane from St. Vincent Healthcare.

On the plane I sat in back facing backwards. Ruth was to my left and behind me towards the front of the plane with three medical attendants giving her their full attention. They had all the equipment that is available in a hospital emergency room, just smaller in size.

The flight went well except for the landing. The third time the wheels hit the pavement the plane finally settled down.

It seems that this happens frequently when there are strong cross winds, as there were that night.

We must have left the Glendive airport about 10:30 PM; I remember looking at the clock in the ambulance once on the ground in Billings on our way to Billings Clinic, and it read 11:24. I was surprised that it was that late. The flight of about 220 miles took fifty minutes.

More tests clarified that Ruth had suffered a ruptured brain aneurysm, otherwise known as a subarachnoid hemorrhage. We were told that this was a weakness in a blood vessel from birth. There was no way to cause it, and no way to prevent it. At this time the blood vessel burst, and blood spilled out onto her brain. A brain does not respond well to blood that is directly on it. Our doctor told me that one out of three who have this injury die immediately. The news for the other two wasn't very encouraging either.

The doctor implanted a monitor to measure the pressure of the fluid on Ruth's brain. Along with the monitor was a drain in the event that the pressure increased beyond what was considered safe. This installation securely wrapped made Ruth look like she had a spike in her head a little left of center and tilted slightly to the left. At that time her heart rate was good, and the pressure on her brain was good as well.

After that procedure was finished, the doctor told me that Ruth would be going to Denver. He believed that she could be helped through use of a coiling procedure, that there was possibility of recovery and some level of normalcy in life (I specifically asked him about this.), and that she would need to go there to have it done. Only some hospitals across the country are equipped to do this. In the morning he would try to make arrangements, and he would probably have the appointment secured by noon.

A friend, Otis, had driven our car to Billings, and he was there to take me to a hotel for the night, or what was left of it. We retired about 4 AM. He set the alarm for 8:30 so that he could get a breakfast tray and bring it up to the room. We slept fitfully at best.

We rose according to plan. While just beginning to eat our breakfast the phone rang. Arrangements were in place to go to Denver, and I was to get back to the hospital as soon as possible; we were to leave in one hour. Our doctor had done his best to get us to the next stage!

We hurried back to the hospital. Actually, we could have taken our time, because we did not leave within an hour. But when we did leave, we had a lovely flight. The weather was beautiful, and I could see snow in the mountains for much of the flight. After seeing us off, Otis returned to Glendive with our car.

The med-flight crew gave me a headset so I could participate in conversation with them. I didn't talk much, but I listened to them bantering back and forth; obviously they knew each other well. I had requested and was given permission to use my laptop computer to write during the flight. I realized that it might be important to document what was happening, and the best way to do that was to write while I remembered.

This time I sat near the front of the plane facing backwards. The two pilots were right behind me. I was on the left side, and Ruth was ahead of me on the right side. Again, three medical attendants gave her their full attention.

This flight lasted about one hour and forty minutes; by ground it is a little more than 550 miles. We landed at Centennial Airport which is significantly closer to Swedish Medical Center than the international airport most travelers use.

After one more ambulance ride, we arrived at Swedish early afternoon, Tuesday, December 20. To get there from home we had ridden in an ambulance on the ground five times and in a fixed wing, twin-engine airplane two times. It was an unusual way to travel since we avoided passenger terminals and security clearances, and one of us was incommunicative on a gurney. I appreciated that Ruth had been well wrapped in blankets to protect from the cold during transitions.

Less than twenty-four hours after the aneurysm ruptured, we were in Denver, about 600 miles from home, with basically the clothes on our backs. I had an overnight bag improperly provisioned, and Ruth had only a hospital gown.

Ruth was on life support all this time. Switching the equipment from hospital to ambulance and later back again required about a half hour each time. I commented that this procedure should be done by someone who was methodical, not necessarily someone who was quick.

Our oldest daughter, Merrily, had already traveled from Minnesota to Denver and was sitting in the Critical Care Unit's waiting room when I arrived.

The team at Swedish was ready for us. We were quickly ushered into a conference room, and the team began discussing with us the possibilities and options.

There were two possible ways of treating Ruth. The team from Swedish hoped they could use the coiling procedure. The surgeon would make a small incision in the groin area, and by traveling through a blood vessel they could insert a titanium coil into the rupture itself. The titanium would coil in upon itself and attract blood platelets which in turn would seal off the rupture.

Not all ruptured aneurysms can be treated this way. If Ruth's could not, they would have to use the clipping procedure, which would involve removing a section of skull and clipping the ruptured area to prevent further bleeding.

Though terribly invasive, this method would allow the surgeon to clean up some of the blood spilled on her brain. Otherwise the normal processes in Ruth's body would have to clean up the blood through osmosis.

The physician talking with us, Dr. Bellon, was the coiling specialist. They would take Ruth directly to examine her. If she was a candidate for coiling, it would be done before we would see him again. If she was not, another doctor would do the clipping either that evening or the next morning.

CHAPTER 2

THE OTHER SIDE OF STAGE ONE (PART 1)

I have to think to know what day it is. I was surprised to walk out of the hospital the other day and see Christmas lights—I guess it is that season.

I have been overwhelmed by the people praying for us and it has been a great comfort. Within minutes of Ruth's initial event, the prayer chains of many churches in Eastern Montana were praying for her. This spread to other states and even countries. The Church, the Body of Christ, has amazing connections! We know of people praying in South America and Asia; who knows about the other continents? I say "Amazing" because we are some insignificant people from insignificant Eastern Montana.

I have been exercised over praying for Ruth. James says that our prayers are not answered because we ask amiss. I may be asking amiss. I may be asking selfishly because I love her dearly and hope that life can eventually be like it was—our life together has been in a way like a dream come true, even better than I hoped when we got married. God's plan is good!

So then I think of the thousands of people praying. They may pray in a more disinterested fashion than I do, and that's good. I will always cherish their involvement.

But then I was impacted deeply by Romans 8:26-27. It says, "And in the same way the Spirit also helps our weakness; for we do not know how to pray as we should, but the Spirit Himself intercedes for us with groanings too deep for words; and He who searches the hearts knows what the mind of the Spirit is, because He intercedes for the saints according to the will of God." So our best prayer warrior is the Holy Spirit Himself. That was a terrific encouragement!

But then this morning as I woke I went back to Romans 8. It's kind of funny in that usually I might concentrate on Romans 8:28, which is also a blessing. But I read on to verse 34, and my socks just about blew off (if they were even on at that time). Guess who else is praying for us: the Lord Jesus Christ Himself! One thing I know, and that is that when the Son of God and the Spirit of God are praying according to the mind of God, that prayer will without a doubt be answered. I don't know what form that final answer will take, but I do know that God will be glorified. It may not always seem like it, but I know in my head that God's grace is sufficient for my need as well as for Ruth's.

from the Care Page

I've been surprised by the number of people who asked me, "How are you doing?" It wasn't just the usual, "How are you?" It was a genuine question about my welfare. Perhaps you wonder the same.

It seemed odd to me that I was suffering; after all, it was Ruth who experienced the physical trauma. But she was sedated for weeks and does not remember about a month's worth of time. I was the one who observed it all. I was the one who called 911. I was the one who made the decisions and signed my name. I was the one who directed many kinds of communications. I was the one who considered possible outcomes. I was the one who was aware that we had been wrenched away from everything that defined our normal life.

It was not immediately clear, but, in looking back, it became obvious to me that God was choreographing everything. And He sent little hints of His care periodically to comfort me.

The first police officer who came into our house was Tim, a man who attended our church. That was comforting. Mary

Jo on the ambulance crew was someone I knew. Another comfort.

I couldn't be with Ruth at the Glendive Medical Center while she was undergoing the CT scan, so I went to the little chapel. I wanted to read in the Psalms. I hadn't been there long when Tim and Delane, a couple from church, walked in. It was wonderful to see them. Tim is an anesthesiologist; he was not on call that evening but came in to help. He took charge of Ruth, preparing her for the trip to Billings. More comfort—I trusted him fully.

Word traveled quickly. Before long a group from church plus three pastors from the area had gathered at the emergency room. Their presence was strengthening. They prayed with me, all quietly, and some out loud. They saw Ruth while she was there because of Tim, our anesthesiologist's efforts. I don't know how the word spread so quickly, but in a very short time half a dozen churches in our community were praying for Ruth plus others in outlying areas of Eastern Montana.

When I was told that we would be going to Billings, I was given three options: I could drive to Billings, someone could drive with me, or I could fly on the plane with Ruth. I believed I was thinking in a collected fashion, and I thought that it might be good therapy for me to drive to Billings. I enjoy driving, and the task on that cool night might be just what I needed to settle my thoughts and emotions.

But Gwen, one of the church ladies, stepped forward and said to me, "Arlie, you are not driving." Later I was thankful she had done that. It seems that one cannot understand his own level of mental command, because to myself I seemed fine, but I was not. So I said I would fly with Ruth. And I'm glad I did.

The hospital staff told me to go back home and pack an overnight bag. Don, from church, went with me. To show how well I was thinking, I failed to pack my shaving kit. It sat on a shelf in the basement bathroom ready to go, but I didn't even think of it. Fortunately, I did think to include my old Mac PowerBook; in time it became a very important communications companion. I also did remember to turn the stove off—the corn chowder was still warming there.

I also forgot my cell phone. That in itself is not a surprise, because I was not accustomed to carrying one except for emergencies. However, I had planned to pack it; I did pack the recharge cord! A couple from our church, Keith and Jeanne, went back to the house to find it and bring it back to the hospital.

Though I didn't process it at the time, later I thought about that instruction. Why was I told to pack just an overnight bag? It was obvious that Ruth would not be coming back to Glendive in the morning. At least she would not be coming back alive. Maybe the medical personnel didn't think it through. Or maybe they believed she would come back in a day or so—for the funeral. I know that some at the hospital that evening really didn't expect to ever see her again alive.

Someone at the hospital—I don't remember who—commented that I didn't seem to understand the gravity of her condition. How did they expect me to act? Should I have yelled, stamped my feet, put a fist through the wall? That would have been out of character for me. If you had been there (and some of you were), you would probably have thought that I seemed about the same as usual. That's probably why someone came to the wrong conclusion.

I did understand! I clearly understood when I found her that any one of her noisy uneven breaths could be the last. I may not have been thinking clearly in some respects, but I did understand that!

Before we left for the airport, the group that had gathered to pray were allowed to individually say "Good-by" to Ruth. They reported to me later some of their conversations and thoughts; they expected that they would never again see Ruth alive. The hospital staff agreed.

I also knew the ambulance driver, Rita, who took us to the local airport. Another bit of comfort.

When we were transported from the airport to the hospital in Billings, one of the flight ambulance crew said he would be praying for us. Still more comfort.

We do not have medical insurance, but for years we have participated in Samaritan Ministries, a Christian medical cost-sharing organization. I knew at some point early in this experience I would need to call them to let them know what had happened. So Tuesday morning I called them from Billings. The man who answered the phone was Ed. I told him what had happened, and here's the gist of what he said, "The last thing you need now is paperwork and money concerns. What you need right now is prayer. Let me pray with you, and shortly after I hang up, hundreds more will be praying for you." It was another comfort. Now I really understood why people join an organization like this.

God was choreographing the unfolding events, but only in retrospect did it become clear that His plan was not for Ruth to die. The injury occurred on a Monday, usually the day of the week that I tuned pianos out of town. I did have some work in a town about fifty miles away, and I was hoping to get caught up on this last Monday before Christmas.

But as I thought through the schedule, none of the jobs seemed to be time sensitive. And that Monday was my birthday. So after contemplating the possibilities, I decided to stay home that day. If I had not been home when Ruth crumpled in the bathroom, she would have died. That was my evaluation, and it was confirmed by medical personnel. God had directed my decision beforehand.

I was also told that I had saved her life by straightening her out on the floor. I certainly did not do it for that reason. It just seemed to be unwise to leave her in a crumpled heap.

And then when Otis drove our car to Billings that night, he had an unusual experience. He suddenly at one point found himself driving in the passing lane on I-94 for no reason of his choosing. But as he crested the next hill, there was a large deer carcass lying in the driving lane. Had he hit it, the car would have been damaged, and he might have become another emergency. (That is why I was discouraged from driving to Billings—one emergency at a time is enough!) God was taking care of him and of our car.

As we were about to leave Billings for Denver Tuesday morning I received an email telling me that our oldest daughter, Merrily, was leaving Minnesota to fly to Billings. That was a problem. She didn't know that we were headed to Denver. So I called our second child and oldest son, Andrae, in California. He simply said that I should not worry, he would take care of it. He told me later that when he had told me that, he had no idea what he would do.

Merrily could have flown directly from Minneapolis to Billings, but she chose a different flight, one that would arrive sooner and be cheaper. And it went through Denver! Andrae contacted her husband, Hans, and he texted her to stay in Denver. Hans' sister Detra lives in Denver, and she could make sure Merrily got to Swedish Medical Center. The two of them were in the Critical Care Unit B's waiting room when I arrived. God was guiding the schedule even before we knew what the schedule was, and He was continuing to provide comfort at each juncture.

I cannot tell you how good it was to see her! If I could almost describe it, I might say that it was kind of like walking through a doorway into a totally strange place and discovering that it was like home! It was a great comfort to see Merrily, and Detra was especially helpful since she is also a nurse—though at another hospital—and was able to orient us to hospital culture.

Perhaps you could say that we were just lucky, that these developments just happened. But I'm not willing to go that route. This was all arranged by a loving God who cares for His own. And I accepted it as such; I hope you do also.

Ruth did show some signs of responsiveness in Billings Tuesday morning. Here is what I wrote in my "Sequence:"

> Ruth was more responsive this morning than any time since yesterday at 5:30. I kissed her on the forehead, and she opened her eyes. Her left hand/arm are limp, but her right hand is strong. Apparently, when they made some kind of contact with her toes, she responded. Her eyes looked like they were alive, and sometimes her

eyebrows moved as if she was trying to figure out something.

Our situation made me think about our entire family. Again in the "Sequence" I wrote the following:

> I pray for Ruth (I know God is working out His perfect will, even though I wonder what that is). I pray for the children—they have their own lives, and they need to take care of their responsibilities.

CHAPTER 3

THE OTHER SIDE OF STAGE ONE (PART 2)

Merry Christmas! We attended a Christmas Eve candlelight service last night 9 PM at … Church. The message had very little of substance, but the Scripture was excellent as always and the music was wonderful.

Yesterday was a difficult day for me. I couldn't be in the room with Ruth very much. She had had a vasospasm, constriction of the blood vessels in the brain, so they had to do an angioplasty. The next couple days hold the highest risk for this, and they may have to do it another time or several. Without the procedure she could have strokes with damage, so the procedure is necessary. Afterwards it took her a while to settle down, and they had to make adjustments of various kinds to get blood pressure to where they wanted it.

We spent over half an hour in the chapel singing Christmas carols. It was a good time.

Daughter Merrily brought along a book by John Piper, their pastor, entitled "The Misery of Job and the Mercy of God." It is an amazing four-chapter poem! What a gift he has! At the end of the first chapter it says this:

"Come, learn the lesson of the rod:
The treasure that we have in God.
He is not poor nor much enticed
Who loses everything but Christ."

Along with that I read 1 Peter yesterday. Let me share this verse, though I only share it as part of a theme in that letter:

"Beloved, do not be surprised at the fiery ordeal among you, which comes upon you for your testing, as though some strange thing were happening to you; but to the degree that you share the sufferings of Christ, keep on rejoicing; so that also at the revelation of His glory, you may rejoice with exultation." (1 Pet. 4:12-13)

What stands out to me is that in the final analysis, it is only Christ and heaven that matters. I can read that, I can understand it, I can teach it; but can I live it? That is the question. Am I strong? Hah! You could push me over with a feather. If there is any strength at all, it is Christ's, because I am reduced to nothing. Perhaps I see more clearly that even beyond what I can grasp, everything I am and have is Christ's. Sometimes He gives it, sometimes He takes it away. From the time this happened Monday, I fully knew even in my shocked state that He is still My Lord and My God. Blessed be His name!

from the Care Page

I had time on the flight to Denver to collect my thoughts, if that were even possible. I did have thoughts; one word, a phrase or a sentence, and some questions. They represented reactions to the present and the possible future. They focused on the core values of life. So I began a list.

Here it is in the order that it came to me:

Instant change
 Knew not at all
  Together plans
 Plans?
In the care of the Good Shepherd
 Sheep die easily
 Many complicated ends
  Simplifying
A team
  Life cut in half is what?
 History
 One-flesh cut in half is what?
Loved
 Loved on another level

Does love strengthen?

Decisions

No decisions

What work?

Can we stop work?

Jesus Christ the same always

This was like a brainstorming session. I wrote down whatever came to mind. Look at it yourself. Maybe you can make sense out of the directions my mind was chasing. Think of it in terms of the life Ruth and I shared and the foundation of faith in the Lord Jesus Christ. Let your imagination be your guide.

CHAPTER 4

STAGE TWO—CRITICAL CARE UNIT AT SWEDISH HOSPITAL

When we next saw Dr. Bellon the afternoon of December 20 he reported that the coiling procedure had been successful. This rupture should no longer be a problem. They had also examined Ruth's entire head and discovered no additional aneurysm, no additional blood vessel weakness which might at some future date rupture and bleed onto the brain.

Ruth was somewhat responsive after the procedure. She even tried to talk to me, but, of course, it was impossible because of the breathing tube in her throat. Quietness in her room was important so as not to excite her.

The major problem had now been remedied. This did not mean Ruth was out of danger, but it did mean that there was now a possibility of recovery.

Probably the most expected complication was that of vasospasms. The brain at some point realizes that the blood from the original bleed is still on the brain. So it responds by constricting the flow of blood through the blood vessels of the brain; its logic is that this bleed must be prevented. It does not recognize that that bleed is old and that the rupture has already been repaired.

Actually at this point the brain needs unrestricted blood flow in order to remove the old blood that is there and to deliver the nutrients for brain function and recovery. So in the vasospasm the brain actually works against itself.

The doctors identify these vasospasms through a TransCranial Doppler scan and treat them through angioplasty. You may think of angioplasty as a balloon treatment to open up blood vessels. It is that, but it can also deliver medicine designed to relax the blood vessel's constriction. Sometimes one treatment might be appropriate, sometimes the other, and sometimes both.

After the coiling procedure there is a four- to fourteen-day window in which vasospasms are most likely, and the likelihood is greatest in the middle of that period. Apparently after that time the brain has become accustomed to its new condition and relaxes to facilitate blood flow.

Sure enough, December 24, four days after the coiling procedure was done, Ruth experienced a vasospasm. After I was informed and signed appropriate papers she was taken away for the angioplasty. After the angioplasty Ruth was restless for a while, so our time together was quite limited that day.

Ruth had another vasospasm and angioplasty Christmas Day and the day after. In fact she had one every day through December 28, but that day they couldn't finish. They tried the application of medicine, and it lowered her blood pressure too much. It was important to keep the blood pressure elevated; that in itself would aid in keeping the blood vessels open. They actually wanted the blood pressure to remain above 140 during this time, and Ruth was mostly able to maintain that on her own.

The December 29 CT scan showed that where the balloon had been used the day before in the front of the brain, the vessels were nicely open. But in the back they looked worse. So the plan was to use the balloon again. The doctor thought she might be 'turning the corner' as far as the vasospasms were concerned.

About December 26 a fever manifested itself in addition to the vasospasms. Repeated cultures taken over several days revealed no infection, but to be safe Ruth's medical providers gave her antibiotics. The conclusion was that the fever was caused simply by the situation in the brain.

Ruth did show signs of responsiveness. December 27 I wrote the following in the 'Sequence:'

> Ruth seemed to make good progress today. She tracks well with her eyes. Her eyebrows furrow as though she is trying to make sense of what is happening around her. She at least once lifted her right hand and arm and even shoulder. She seemed to try to smile once, and even the day nurse commented on that.

She did not respond well to commands, but she was moving some of her limbs at times and in ways of her own whether by choice or involuntarily. Any movement was welcomed by us as a good sign.

The morning of December 27 the day nurse, Michelle, asked if we wanted to see the CT scan pictures. Of course, we did! She showed us pictures from early in this experience as well as the last ones taken. It was obvious even to our untrained eyes that the spilled blood was being removed and that the brain's shapes were beginning to reappear.

By December 31 the vasospasms were continuing. That day they used a combination of balloon and medicine. They applied a medicine to maintain blood pressure, and the result was good.

Every morning the medical team, usually composed of five people, would meet in front of Ruth's room and discuss her condition and progress. Whichever family members were with me at the time and I were invited to be a part of the conference and even to ask questions. Our questions focused on clarifications and expectations. The morning of December 31 we were told that two blood clots had been discovered.

One of the blood clots was in her right arm—that one was not a major concern. The other was in her left calf; it was a concern. She was given blood thinner to hopefully avoid a stroke. Blood thinner was not really desirable in view of the coiling seal, but by this time it perhaps would not be a problem. And any therapeutic exercising was limited to limbs not containing clots. At the same time non-exercise is a condition in which clots prosper, so she wore pressure stockings and massaging 'boots.' This concern continued throughout her hospital stay.

During this period of time Ruth did not look like herself except from her nose up (even that means disregarding the spike on her head!). She was badly swollen. This was intentional. She needed an increased amount of fluid in her body just to increase blood flow to the brain so repair could continue. We were told that when this period came to an end, the swelling would quickly subside.

January 1 was an exciting day! When we arrived, we immediately noticed that the breathing tube had been removed! Now Ruth looked more like herself, and the processes of swallowing and talking could again begin. I went to Starbucks in the nearby Safeway store to celebrate with coffee and Very Berry coffee cake, and I felt like telling everyone I met that her breathing tube was out! Just to put you at ease, you should know that I did restrain myself.

The excitement continued. That day her central drip (neck I-V) and her camino (brain monitor and drain that looked like a spike in her head) were removed. The exposed area of her head revealed very short hair and a suture. But she was beginning to look much more normal after almost two weeks.

Ruth still could not feed herself or even swallow, so nutrition was provided now via NG (nasogastric tube), a tube that goes through the nose to the stomach. That was a vast improvement over all the equipment that had been attached.

That day also Ruth indicated that she wanted some glasses. She used inexpensive reading glasses of various strengths at home, so we bought some for her. She appeared to be trying to figure out everything around her. She would even try to pucker up when I threw kisses to her.

Everything was looking so good that talk of rehabilitation began in earnest!

January 2 Ruth and I watched the Nebraska/South Carolina Capital One bowl game together. She slept through parts of it, but she shook her head in disappointment whenever she saw the Cornhuskers make a bad play.

There were setbacks. Early in her Swedish hospital experience tests showed some weakness of her heart. It did not seem to affect the heart's functioning, but there was concern again on January 3. And at this point her lungs were collecting too much fluid.

Not only that, but vasospasms returned. They were supposed to have ended by now. One could hope that they would not require intervention, but it was unsettling. Merrily wrote that day for the Care Page:

> We are tempted to ask why the vasospasms continue; after all, the medical staff said they should only occur in the 4-14 day window after the aneurysm. We are at day 15. Why longer Lord?

Anticipation was building at a rapid clip over the past couple of days as Mom began to emerge from the fog of the trauma. It was easy to start mapping out the road to recovery (a couple more days in the hospital, some rehab in Denver which would culminate in a trip back to Montana, with more rehab to follow there. . .) The countdown was on. After all, why lie around and wait?!

CHAPTER 5

THE OTHER SIDE OF STAGE TWO (PART 1)

Off and on these days, I have been thinking about angels. In a figurative way I could call 'angels' all those who have helped her from the first responders all the way to the medical personnel here and those who have come alongside us. (Even yesterday we received offers of help from some in the Denver area and beyond who have some connection to us.) But I'm thinking of the real angels, not the 'Touched-by-an-Angel' variety. Hebrews 1:14, in a book whose purpose is to show that Jesus is superior to anyone you can put up alongside Him, says this of angels: "Are they not all ministering spirits, sent out to render service for the sake of those who will inherit salvation?" And to ask the question is to answer it. Yes!

Just to set a stage here, you remember that angels were very much involved in Job's experience. In fact, it was the prince of the dark angels, Satan, who began the challenge against Job. And you may also remember that angels were very much involved in the most horrific suffering of all time, the crucifixion of Jesus in which He paid for the sins of the world for those who believe Him.

So, how are the angels ministering to Ruth and to us? I have not seen them in the room, but on the basis of God's word I know they are there. Maybe they are helping the medical personnel—I can't really claim too much there. But I am confident that they are looking at these people around the world who are weeping and praying for Ruth. Then they are looking at God and wondering what He is going to do. And as His purposes in this wrenching experience unfold, they will break into songs like you've never heard in praise to our heavenly Father.

from the Care Page

Swedish Medical Center in Denver has four Critical Care Units. Ruth was in "B" which specializes in brain injury. We could open the CCU door, look all the way down the corridor past the nurses's station right into her room and see whether there was activity in her room. If you came for a visit, you walked straight ahead down the hall and eventually into her room.

Some of you who read this know what it is to spend time in a critical care unit. If you never have, this should give you some idea of what it is like.

Ruth was connected to a variety of machines. We could read the continuous output of data including breathing, pulse, blood pressure, and brain pressure. We had a quick course in the significance of numbers, what range was acceptable and what was not. And there were also the I-Vs to provide nutrition and medicines.

My idea of a successful day was to sit with her as much as possible. That turned out to be less than I had expected at times. Visiting hours were from 8 AM to 8 PM. There was to be no visiting from 2:30 PM to 4:30 PM. Often the morning was limited as well because that was usually when Ruth received an angioplasty. We did attempt to be there regularly by late morning so as not to miss the team meeting held outside her door.

These meetings were informational for us since that was the time Ruth's condition and progress were discussed. Jason, the daytime nurse those first few days, was especially helpful to us. He had a gift for explaining through illustrations what was happening to Ruth. He explained that brain recovery is unpredictable. He said Ruth could possibly wake up and not know who she was, she could wake up and quickly return to whatever she had been before, or she could wake up and need months of therapy. He was also very kind as he gave his attention to Ruth.

It was in those meetings that we learned the seriousness of Ruth's condition. In the words of Dr. Warner, the critical care specialist, her condition upon arrival had been a "5." When I asked what that meant, she replied that scale was "1" to "5" (with 5 being the worst). Yet they maintained that her general health was excellent. They also told us that we needed to look after our own wellbeing; at first we wouldn't be able to help Ruth much, but later her need for our presence would increase.

We had purchased a cell phone a couple years ago mainly for emergency use. Now I gave its number out to the medical personnel frequently as they needed to be able to contact me when there were changes or if they needed my permission for a procedure. We were called the first time in the wee hours of December 21 because Ruth's response to commands had been slow. So they did another CT scan. The nurse who called said she really wouldn't have had to because Ruth's responses had been brisk again even before the scan. But she called because she had said she would. We appreciated the medical personnel following through on their word even though it meant answering the phone during the night. That cell phone became a very useful tool in talking to people at the hospital, people back home, family, and others, some even in other countries.

Merrily and I stayed the first few nights at the Marriot Hotel, which provided a Swedish Hospital discount. It was a pleasant place, and the kindness of people there encouraged us. We traveled back and forth in the shuttle, and even the driver was kind and comforting.

Our son Andrae arrived from California December 21. He had rented a car, so now our travel became more efficient. Two days later Merrily's husband, Hans, and, Collin, a Chinese student friend of theirs, arrived.

At that point we transferred lodging to Detra and Mark's house. Their house was large, and we could stay there without causing too much upheaval in their lives. I immediately slept better, and we began to have more home-like meals since we could now do some of our own cooking. I usually lament the shortness of time when in a city with restaurants too many to sample, but we had plenty of chances to eat out. But when there for an extended stay, it is better to manage one's diet.

December 22 we enjoyed a sizable snowstorm which left a foot of snow on the ground. I didn't mind since I didn't have to move it. Andrae made the most of it by constructing a snowman in the backyard that was about six feet tall! In a few days the head fell off and a few days later not much was left—warm weather had again triumphed. I thoroughly appreciated his zest for life in building that snowman.

I received word from home that a lady from our church, Donna, would be coming to Denver to spend Christmas with family. She was offering to bring along clothes and other items I needed from home. I have to admit I was a little tired of doing laundry in the sink every night and wearing the same clothes each day, and I would sleep better in my own pajamas. So via cell phone I directed several people throughout the house back home, up and down stairs, to find what I needed. What a blessing it was when she appeared December 23 along with her grandson and his girlfriend and the items I needed! I was now getting settled in for the duration.

We received an invitation to meet a couple who worked in ministry very near Swedish. We had known Paul and Helen and their families previously. It was very encouraging to walk to their offices, talk, and pray together. The same evening we were able to visit in the home of a nephew in a suburb. It was good to see the normalcy of Cassidy and Katrina's home and family.

The day after Christmas I had a nice visit with Adisa, our nurse. I asked her if Ruth might be able to dream during her sedation. Adisa said there is not proof she cannot, so her conclusion was that she probably could. I decided that if she possibly could, I would pray for Ruth to have sweet dreams. This put me on a mission. Later I asked another nurse, and she said definitely not. The portion of the brain that involves dreaming had been injured. Later yet another said she simply did not know. So the definitive answer was unavailable. The answers I got depended on whom I asked. In asking Ruth later about this, she has no recollection whether she dreamed or not, and she had no visions or other supernatural experiences to share. So the jury remains out.

Hans and Merrily expressed concern that our third child and second daughter, Renessa, in Central Asia was having difficulty processing all this so far away. Perhaps we could get someone from the hospital to talk to her. The morning of December 27 Ruth again had Michelle as her day nurse. When we told her our request, she offered to talk to Renessa and did so almost immediately. We were amazed at her ability to quickly summarize Ruth's situation from day one. It was as though she had prepared to give this report. (We believe the Lord even appointed the specific nurse for each day's work.) We also learned that Ruth's rupture had been 6 mm, and the more common were 1 or 2 mm. To our delight Michelle said that Ruth would not die from this!—that was the first time we had heard that. But she also said that the level of recovery was unknown at that point.

December 28 Ruth's oldest brother came to visit. Harv and his wife Marj lived about an hour away. Their comfort meant much to us as they had tragically lost their son some years before. Their daughter and her family also came along. They visited on two more occasions while we were there.

The following day we were invited to the home of a childhood friend, Juanita. She and her husband, Dennis, were gracious hosts with food, conversation, and offers of help. It was a blessing to me to see them after many years; they are godly people who have served many others.

Hans, Merrily, and Collin had to leave December 31. But the same day Carmody (youngest child and second son) and his wife Christy arrived from Arizona. They would be with us for one week.

Then January 2 an Air Force Lieutenant, Brad, and his family stopped to see us. We had known him since he was a little boy. Kendra, his wife, had family about an hour away, so on their way home from Christmas vacation they stopped to see us. I was again blessed as he gathered us in a circle and prayed for us.

On the same day a Bible college friend, roommate, and fellow quartet member, Jim, drove eight hours one way to see us on his day off. I really didn't think it was reasonable for him to come that far, but he wanted to. I couldn't say "No." He took us out for supper and insisted we choose a dinner, not a sandwich! Then he visited with Ruth and showed her a PowerPoint presentation of his family. She indicated she recognized them. After praying with us he returned home to Kansas where he was currently a pastor. We were again overwhelmed with his display of love to us.

You can imagine rightly that all of these people were like angels to us. The touch of their lives on ours was strengthening.

CHAPTER 6

THE OTHER SIDE OF
STAGE TWO (PART 2)

Yesterday was a busy day—going strong from 6:30 AM until after 11:00 PM.

It was a people day. Before we left for the hospital, St. David called from Brazil. He nourished me with truth from Job and prayed for us. Later as we were about to leave the hospital for a bit, I practically ran into St. Thomas in the hall. He is the pastor of the church we visited last Sunday, and he and his associate had come to see us. Then we spent a precious time with Sts. Paul and Helen. We knew they lived here, but had not realized their offices are only four or five blocks from Swedish Hospital. Our visit with them was encouraging and helped us to focus on the Lord. I am not exaggerating—those folks are saints, set apart to God and serving others in His name!

Our people day was not yet done. After our hospital time was done for the day, we went to my nephew's house to see him, his dear wife, and their two-month-old baby. The older two children were in bed. Great to see them and their family!

It's interesting that being with people yesterday made for a full and lively day. Yet I wonder if it is easy to let people take the place of God. The verse I have been thinking about overnight is Psalm 73:25-26.

"Whom have I in heaven but Thee? And besides Thee, I desire nothing on earth. My flesh and my heart may fail, but God is the strength of my heart and my portion forever."

When you are removed from the daily routine of things, schedules, and responsibilities, the expression of verse 25 becomes absolutely clear. I believe it, but I can get distracted. To know that ultimately it is God and me only is truly the greatest comfort. In the final analysis, God and you alone is true. That may bother some people, but when you know God through His Son, the only Mediator, you also know that you are enveloped in the unmeasurable love of God.

from the Care Page

You might envision me spending day and night by Ruth's side encouraging her and constantly noting the monitors. That was certainly part of it but by no means all of it.

My time was not totally devoted to giving Ruth attention. I was on assignment to write Sunday School lesson plans for a publishing company. I contemplated requesting an extension, since I really didn't know if I could finish on time. Again through use of the phone, I directed Dick, a man from our church back home, in the process of emailing files to me and later printing some files and sending them, so that I could continue the assignment. I also had to purchase a new-to-me draw program that I could use to create the illustrations needed. So I was able to continue working even in Ruth's room sometimes with iTunes playing sacred instrumental music softly in the background. I did finish the assignment and mailed it in on time!

We had responsibilities back home in the church and out from the church as well. Various people graciously offered to substitute for us usually even before we made request. The chairman of our church board told me my job was to care for Ruth—they would take care of everything else. And they did! I was overwhelmed by God's love demonstrated through them.

January 2 when Ruth was somewhat awake we were able to skype with Andrae and family in California and with Sy, Renessa, and family a half-world away. The connection was not always good, but Ruth recognized everyone and afterwards whispered, "That's great!"

We really appreciated the medical personnel who worked with Ruth. Each one was like an angel to us. I was, however, almost thrown out of the hospital one day. As I noted earlier, I was not accustomed to cell phone use. So one day it rang while I was in Ruth's room. I looked for a place to talk where I would not disturb others. Well, apparently my choice of places did not suffice, because the nurse on duty became upset with me. She threatened to throw me out because my noise-making might be retarding the recovery of everyone in the unit!

This same nurse insisted that we be very quiet so as not to arouse Ruth. Yet she would ask whether I were reading to Ruth yet. That suggestion seemed at odds with her other insistence. Since we were not very pleased with her, we decided to get even. In the corridor that branched off to the left as one exited Ruth's room there was a bed with a manikin on it. (We learned later that it was being used for instructional purposes.) I was rather shocked when I first saw it. Since our nurse was so concerned with the vibes we were emitting, we decided to draw her attention to the manikin the next time she was on duty and suggest that it was affecting Ruth's condition negatively. In the providence of God, Ruth never had that nurse again. It was probably better for her and us that way!

Hans was given the task of finding a Christmas Day service for us to attend. Christmas was on Sunday, and the resulting oddity was that many churches had no services that day. But he did find one at Hillcrest Christian Reformed Church. We went and found it to be by divine appointment.

We arrived early because we had mistaken information as to the starting time. But even that was ordained of the Lord. Because we were early we were able to meet Pastor Tom and a few other people. The service that morning could not have been more fitting had they known we were coming! It was uplifting to us. We returned there every Sunday we were in Denver. That church was very loving and became another group of prayer warriors!

The music was excellent there as well. We have always been involved with music on various levels. December 24 our little family sang carols for half an hour in the hospital chapel. I love to sing, and I love to sing the carols, but I could hardly sing. I couldn't get enough breath to sing an entire phrase. And the songs affected me so strongly that at one point I had to remove myself from our small group and weep. When they finished the song Hans came over and prayed for me so that I was strengthened.

It seems odd, perhaps, but in that suffering we realized the love and goodness of God like we never had before. It was expressed by many people. Within a few days of Ruth's injury we were aware of people praying on at least five continents. Thousands of prayers were ascending daily on Ruth's behalf. We wondered and discussed what it must be like in heaven when the Body of Christ is aroused on behalf of one of its own. Of course we know that this happens often with others even when we ourselves might be unaware of it. Now we were in the middle of it, and we were just some basically unknown people from Eastern Montana!

The evening of December 20 our local church in Glendive hosted a prayer vigil for two hours. People could come and go, pray, have coffee, visit. They reported a precious time as they were able to share with each other and commit Ruth's condition to God.

Dave, a missionary in South America, called December 27. He prayed with me and shared with me from his teaching at the school there. He had been teaching the poetic books of the Old Testament. The book of Job records the suffering of Job brought on by Satan's attacks. Dave related that God took under His sovereignty all the suffering brought on by Satan. That was a great encouragement to me. I knew that God was involved in our situation, and it was nourishing to be reminded of His superintendence of it all.

The waiting room right outside that CCU was a grim place. Families waited there as the lives of their loved ones hung in the balance. We shared some and together rejoiced when someone had good news. And we all did want good news!

From the beginning various Scriptures came to mind. And I wondered how to pray. I wanted Ruth back just like she had been previously. But was that selfish? Should I not be able to pray in disinterested fashion: "Your will be done"? Perhaps others could pray more objectively. I was drawn to Romans

8 where verse 26 says, "And in the same way the Spirit also helps our weakness; for we do not know how to pray as we should, but the Spirit Himself intercedes for us with groanings too deep for words." I was encouraged because I knew He would pray according to the mind and will of God. God's will would be done, and He would be glorified.

At the suggestion of a friend, and after Andrae had done some research, we established a web site on Care Pages, and it was appropriately called "Romans826." Before this we had emailed the church back home and fielded individual emails, but now we could report to a larger audience more efficiently. I was blessed as I wrote almost daily entries, and the responses from people, some of whom we did not even know, were very strengthening. On occasion one of our children would write the daily post.

The third night in Denver I had a troubling dream. The outcome for Ruth was bad: it appeared that she died. Dreams have a way of being illogical, and this one was no different. In the course of the dream she somehow came back home, and even in my sleep I reasoned that these events did not agree with the way Swedish Medical Center handled matters.

So I concluded that the dream was not true, but rather a test sent from the devil to torment me. How did I respond? I asked the church back home to pray for my thoughts and dreams. I needed to practice Philippians 4:7: "And the peace of God, which surpasses all comprehension, shall guard your hearts and your minds in Christ Jesus." Their prayers were answered; I had no such dreams again.

Almost from the first my mind had been tossing around the possible outcomes. How could I deal with this outcome or that? I could see myself welcoming Ruth back to her former level of function. I contemplated various levels of handicap, and I committed myself to caring for her even if that meant resigning from every obligation we now had.

But what if I lost her? I knew in my head that God's grace would be sufficient even for that, but I could not process it. Thinking of that possibility was devastating: I could not see how our ministry could continue—she and I were a team. I really couldn't even see how life could continue—our way of life and our plans were for us two, not just me. I did not have the resources to face it, not even the faith. I was stripped to nothing. I tried to say, "Not my will but Thine be done," but my heart wasn't in it.

I don't know if it was a dream or a vision, but somehow in that hour I saw the name "JESUS" spelled out in slanted block letters. I was made aware that He Himself was with me. His presence was reassuring but also thoroughly humbling. It was made clear to me that He was with me not because of anything I had done, not because of who I was, and not even because of my faith. He cared for me and would care for me simply because I belonged to Him. It was an unforgettable lesson.

CHAPTER 7

STAGE THREE—NEURO UNIT RECOVERY AT SWEDISH HOSPITAL (PART 1)

The vasospasm threat of the day before did not prevent a move from the third floor to the seventh, room 331. In fact, the vasospasms subsided and did not return!

The transfer took place January 4, and the next day therapists came to evaluate. Ruth needed to learn to swallow, to talk out loud, to sit up, to stand, just about everything. They expected progress as she would 'emerge' more and more.

Ruth had been sedated for a long time, but now she was free to wake up. She did emerge as time went by and could carry on a whispering conversation with those who came. One of those days she viewed pictures of Christy and Ella (our granddaughter) on Carmody's computer. She knew who they were and enjoyed it very much. (Yet today she remembers nothing at all of being in Denver. Even the memory of a few days past that time is gone.)

I had little to no understanding of the muscle tone that was lost. We were told that 10 percent of one's muscle tone is lost every day of non-activity in bed. That means that even the ability to sit up is lost. In effort to regain that, the therapists began by having Ruth sit up with the help of the hospital bed. The first time they did it, they wanted Ruth to be 'up' for at least one half hour; she lasted 1.5 hours. We said all along that when Ruth had the challenge of therapy before her, she would accept the challenge, and she did!

Some of her communicating was done via facial expression. We never knew her eyebrows could say so much! They were helpful in communicating recognition, surprise, amusement, and frustration. She hadn't swallowed yet, but the therapists would be addressing that. So she was still connected to the NG tube for nutrition. But it was a nuisance for her, and I could not blame her for that. She said it felt 'unnatural' and 'like rubber.'

Carmody and Christ had stayed a week, and they needed to return home to work and to two-year-old Ella. So they left January 7. But January 6 Merrily returned for another week.

She had taught school for fifteen years and never taken a day of sick leave. It was especially nice, I thought, that she could take sick leave to help care for her mother at this time. She learned from the therapists and worked Ruth's limbs from time to time, helping wake up the connection between brain and muscles and restore muscle tone.

About this time we learned of something rather strange. It seemed humorous on one level, but it should never have happened, and in the long run it caused a fair amount of frustration. I have an aunt with the same name as my wife. She isn't the same age, doesn't live in the same place, and is not married. But her insurance providers began receiving bills for my Ruth's expenses. Once the bills had been paid, it became difficult to have them unpaid so that the bill could be properly redirected. One would think that could not happen with the HIPAA laws of privacy in place today. We eventually traced the source of the confusion to someone in Billings Clinic. They since have written letters of apology. We understand the hospital also had to pay a fine.

But we continued to experience the goodness and generosity of others. Dennis and Juanita, a couple we had known from long ago from Montana, lived not far from Swedish Medical Center, and they loaned me a Chevy Blazer for the remainder of our time there. I had ridden with others for so long that it was like gaining a new freedom. Its four-wheel-drive capability was useful since the weather blessed us with slick streets a couple days.

Ruth was showing signs of progress, but at this time there was much she could not do. The therapists tried to have her sit on the edge of the bed and even stand, and she couldn't do either. Of course, they were there to protect her and were trying to evaluate just exactly what she could do. I wrote this on the January 6 Care Page:

> Today Ruth is asking questions. She is now beginning to grasp what happened and is happening. I don't think she understands it all now yet. She does remember going to the coffee shop in Wibaux December 19. We are thinking she may be a bit younger when she comes out of this. I asked her this morning how old she was, and she thought maybe about fifty-eight. I'll take it!

When Merrily returned, she brought with her various activities that Ruth might do. You could just see the teacher in Merrily! She helped Ruth make a timeline and lists of family birthdays, anniversaries, locations, etc. We rejoiced as Ruth's memory came back.

One of Ruth's favorite activities was reading. It was fun to watch television and see her read in her whisper voice the text going across the bottom.

January 7 provided excitement for us as Ruth was put into a high back wheel chair. Therapist Paula was hoping Ruth could survive a half hour. We were supposed to watch so that as soon as her neck could no longer hold up her head, we would notify the nurses and put her back to bed. Well, she sat in that chair more than three hours that afternoon, and her head never drooped!

That weekend was a Broncos/Steelers game. We were fans of Tim Tebow, the Broncos quarterback, and he had been quite effective taking control of the latter portions of a number of games so that the Broncos were now in the playoffs. But oddly enough, Ruth decided not to root for Tim. Who knows why? The Broncos won with a great play in overtime. I guess they could win even without Ruth rooting for the quarterback!

January 8 was a big day. Here is an extended excerpt from Merrily's daily email to the family:

> I was able to do the full range of stretches with Mom late this morning and more leg stretches this evening. After watching the physical therapist, I have more ideas about how she would like Mom to be able to move. My opinion is that Mom does need acute therapy and would be able to work for 3 hours per day. I don't say this because Mom is naturally progressing quickly but because I think she has the potential to progress rapidly with the right care. (This of course is not an educated opinion.) The

physical therapist mentioned that we want to get more movement going on the right side to build her strength. I think Mom will also try to make the left side mimic the right side if she can.

Mom likes to read. Robbin … had sent a card yesterday, and Mom read portions of that today. Dad read to her from Romans 8 tonight so I wrote one of the key verses on construction paper and taped it to the bottom of her TV. Mom looked at the verse, read it aloud several times, and made comments on the verse.

It is hard to know what connects for Mom between days or between different parts of the same day. However, within a conversation, she really makes sense. For instance, she told me that "Sometimes we don't know what is important." I asked her what is important, and she said "Life and giving birth." Then she said, "If my mom hadn't given birth, I wouldn't be here."

A really cute moment was when Dad was talking to her bending over the bed and called himself a rascal. She reached up with her index finger and touched the end of his nose in a joking gesture that I have seen in the Rauch household before. :)

Uncle Harvey and Aunt Marj came this afternoon for about an hour. Mom knew who they were right away. Toward the end of the conversation, Uncle Harvey was sharing a childhood memory of Mom, and she really smiled, kind of laughing.

Aside from getting muscle tone back into her body and keeping flexibility in her muscles, the speaking/swallowing area is another big area. Mom says her voice doesn't hurt. We talked to her about the need to talk so she can start eating food.

Later in the day, we tried to see if she could hum. She tried but said she "Couldn't find a pitch." She talked about drinking coffee today and used a marker to print the word "coffee" on a lined notebook page. The c was perfect, and she made the correct motions for all of the other letters although they ended up a little small. (She always does write small!) She had great placement on the line. She also whisper spelled the word as she completed it.

I also wrote in the Sequence:

> We were having some fun at one point when she laid her right hand on my cheek and said, "I have to take care of my honeybunch!" She was wanting to make some 'savory muffins' to give to a friend (Robbin) who sent a card.

> She notices on the board on the wall a space for "Discharge Date" and asked when that will be. We answered the best we could since none of us knows. Then she was wondering how she could prepare for that. We have told her she has one task only, and that is to do as she is told and exercise her discipline to increase her abilities. She is trying.

> We cheered again yesterday as she moved her left arm for the first time, all the fingers on her left hand, and her left thumb and index finger together.

She was frequently asking what the plan was or what her job was. So we eventually made the goal more specific. Merrily made a poster for her that said, "Ruth has one job. Learn to talk. (Speak at high decibels.)" She read the poster and discussed in whispers what it meant.

The next day we came in to discover that she had dislodged her NG. She looked really normal with that out, but she wasn't ready yet to have it out. The tube irritated her. We don't know whether she worked consciously at removing it. Unfortunately, installing it again was difficult. The end somehow did not go down at first but went into her sinuses. It was very difficult for me to watch this as it made her cry.

Even that may have had a silver lining, because after that bit of trauma we heard her real voice for the first time. It wasn't loud, but it was her voice! Apparently that difficulty jolted her into actually using her voice. That was good news, because talking and swallowing are in some ways related. And being able to eat real food would be a huge step forward!

She did something else really special that day. Merrily held a hymnal near her, and on a pillow on her lap she 'played' with correct fingering the right hand parts for that song. I wouldn't have recognized whether the fingering was correct, but Merrily plays as well, and she knew what it was. She was even reaching the correct intervals.

Ruth's left arm was put into a sling whenever she would be moved or be 'up.' The muscles around that shoulder were quite weak, and the fear was that she might cause further injury.

Ruth was often organizing. When we asked for what she was preparing we discovered that she was preparing for

Christmas parties. After all, in her mind we had not yet had Christmas. That reality was difficult for her to grasp.

She also had deep theological thoughts. In one of those thoughtful times, she said, "Only God can give you the motivation to be what He wants you to be." Merrily wrote that on a poster and put it on the wall. That way Ruth and anyone else in the room could read it again. It was an important concept.

She also saw "John 3:16" on a squeeze ball and quoted the verse word-perfect.

Jan 10 Dr. Elliot's assistant, Tyler, talked with us about Ruth's discharge. She should be released to enter acute therapy somewhere. So discussions and research began. Suggestions also came from other sources. Tyler said they wanted her swallowing before she would leave. And he said her recovery was faster than the schedule they had anticipated.

The speech therapist was the one who worked with swallowing. That was surprising at first to me, but the speaking and swallowing mechanisms are related, so they tend to recover together. Sometimes the therapist attached four electrodes to Ruth's neck and attempted to stimulate swallowing and speaking that way. They also first fed her some apple sauce. That was a good choice, not only because of the consistency of the food, but also because Ruth likes it. And she did enjoy that! Several days before she had failed a swallowing test. They were planning to soon give her another, and we hoped she would do better this time.

Sometimes Ruth would say something like, "You are so amazed, but I'm not." We always cheered and congratulated her for some new movement or any new evidence of recovery. But she was thinking about what she had done in the past, and beginning again to do something she had done in the past simply was not impressive to her. But then, she had not seen herself in the condition we had only weeks earlier.

Other people continued to encourage us. One lady came in every day to clean, and she told me one day that she always prayed for Ruth. She also said that our room was full of love. I thought much about that. I don't know what was in other rooms, but it is true that our family members all loved each other, and over all was the love of our heavenly Father. It was also obvious to us that as Ruth woke up more and more, the Holy Spirit was demonstrating His fruit in and through her. He was never absent.

January 11 when we arrived Ruth announced to us that she had fallen. That was not good news. She was also thinking she needed to get up to use the bathroom, so she had simply climbed out of bed. Of course, she did not need to because of catheters. But in her mind that was the proper course of action. She didn't understand that she couldn't stand or walk. When I took her for a ride in the wheel chair, she talked of hopping out. It was funny on one hand, dangerous on another, and it revealed her state of mind.

While Merrily worked with her on making a timeline since her injury, she commented that "God has provided for us." It was a true statement, and yet she really had little grasp of all the ways He had provided for us.

The occupational therapist worked with her sitting on the edge of the bed. The day before she could sit about forty seconds without help. Today it was over a minute. She was getting stronger.

The speech therapist gave her grape nectar this time, and she was able to drink that. These drinks are called nectar because they are thickened. The epiglottis works too slowly to handle thin liquids, but it can process the nectar as muscular ability returns.

CHAPTER 8

STAGE THREE—NEURO UNIT RECOVERY AT SWEDISH HOSPITAL (PART 2)

We arrived January 12 to discover that Ruth had been moved to room 322 because of her fall. Now she was right across from the nurses' station so they could keep better watch. They also provided a lower bed so that if she did get out, the fall would be less dangerous. Also, she was given a yellow night gown. And there was a yellow sock hanging on her door. That was nice because yellow is Ruth's favorite color. But we learned that yellow in the hospital is a code. It means that the patient is a fall risk. It's a good thing Ruth likes yellow!

She was worried that the people around her would think she was lazy. She also thought that if she didn't get up to walk, she would lose the ability to walk. What she couldn't process was that she had already lost the ability to walk and needed to gain that back very slowly and carefully.

The nurses put mittens on her hands so that she would not pull out that irritating NG. Well, she somehow removed them and pulled out the NG anyway. How did she do it? She used her teeth. One evening after the mittens had been put on Merrily and I went to the cafeteria to eat. We returned forty-five minutes later and the mittens were off. She said, "Everyone is so interested in these mittens, but I'm not." The staff began calling her Houdini because their efforts to keep her safe were somewhat ineffective.

Sometimes in making her Christmas plans she thought her parents would be coming to visit. This unsettled me a bit, because they had died about twenty years before. But I would explain it to her, and she seemed to accept it well. The ritual of providing that explanation was repeated several times on different days. In these Christmas plans she was still planning to have people come to our home. Earlier she had been interested in making savory muffins. Now that changed to savory pancakes. I don't know why she was so stuck on "savory" as the proper adjective for food. I had never known her to make use of that word, but it was her favorite now.

Ruth thought she shouldn't be the center of attention. That was her true personality showing again. But I told her she was a queen for now and everyone enjoyed serving her. I'm not sure what she thought of that.

Discussion continued about moving to acute therapy somewhere. Would it be in Denver, or could we do it closer to home? The doctors told us that if she was well enough to be moved somewhere else in Denver, she would also be well enough to be moved to Montana. So after thorough discussion and research, we made application to New Hope Rehabilitation which is part of St. Vincent Hospital in Billings, Montana. We had received very good reports from others whose family members had spent time there. What surprised me was that the doctors spoke as if I could drive her back to Montana in my car. I really didn't think that would be possible.

But to prepare, Merrily and I went shopping. Ruth had absolutely no clothes of her own in Denver; she had arrived in a hospital gown. We went to some second-hand stores and some retail stores. The result was several outfits that would look nice and be comfortable. We were sure she would approve the prices we paid, since she watches that very closely.

January 13 the occupational therapist had Ruth put on a pair of pants. The exercise was good in itself as she guided Ruth and had Ruth do as much of it as she could by herself.

But once she had them on, she felt free to sit in various jaunty postures that would have been immodest otherwise. For example, she would pull her feet close to her torso with her knees pointing up and then one leg flopping to the side; this would not have been a modest 'skirt' posture.

A couple times she asked questions that caught me off guard. That day she asked me if Arlie was with Klines. So I asked her who I was. Her answer was that I was her husband. (Fortunately, she never wavered in that knowledge.) Then I asked her what my name was. She said it was Arlie. So I must not have been with Klines after all! And in that moment she was satisfied.

I had the privilege of accompanying Ruth when she was given the barium swallowing test. I had to wear a lead apron. On a screen I could see what was happening. She was given some solid food. I observed some movement, and quickly the food went down. She passed the entire test except the thin liquid portion. I could see it dripping off the epiglottis. But she did well enough that her menu was greatly expanded, and she could begin to order food for meals.

During the test I could see some of her teeth on the screen and also some vertebrae. I noticed something the approximate shape of a bean. I inquired whether that was something in her or something in the machine. The answer? It was a snap on her gown!

For lunch that day she had cream of wheat, peaches, and jello. And she fed herself! For supper she had cheese burger patty, butternut squash, and tapioca pudding. These foods were pureed, but they smelled and tasted good.

That evening Hans called to talk to Merrily. Merrily gave the phone to Ruth and she was able to whisper to Hans. Well, that was the start of something. So later Andrae called me, and I gave the phone to Ruth. She began talking out loud to him and to our grandson Josiah! Recovery often seemed like that. She wouldn't do it for the therapist, though I think she tried, but when she decided to do it on her own, she did!

Finally January 14 the NG came out. Ruth still was not able to eat enough nutrition on her own, so they installed a PEG. PEG is short for percutaneous endoscopic gastrostomy. Now, aren't you glad they call it a PEG? This tube goes right into the stomach about an inch above the navel. It is installed from the inside out. Medicine or food can be poured directly into the stomach. Once it is installed it must remain at least thirty days. We learned that some people who cannot swallow use these for years.

Romans 8:26 had been so important to me, and Merrily had made a poster with the words from that verse: "The Spirit intercedes for us." Ruth asked Merrily one day how that related to the aneurysm. So Merrily told her that the Spirit was praying for her even during the aneurysm. Then Ruth asked whether the Holy Spirit could not have prevented the aneurysm. What a question! Perhaps that is a subject for another day, but of course He could have. That He didn't indicates that this was part of God's plan for us, and He was using it for His glory.

One night when a nurse came into the room, she looked around and asked Ruth if she was a Christian. We know that at least one night nurse was a believer, and others were certainly aware of God-consciousness in that room.

That Saturday I took Merrily to the airport. Ruth was scheduled to be discharged Tuesday morning, January 17. I would be her only family caretaker there those last couple days.

Tyler, the physician's assistant whom we had come to appreciate and enjoy, came by that day again. He said that patients with her kind of injury were often still in critical care at this time, and here we were planning to leave in a few days. His comment was just one more reminder of God's great goodness to us.

That day Ruth had a special visitor. Her cousin, Cynthia, whom she had not seen in decades, came to visit. They are actually fairly close in age. It was fun to observe them visiting and catching up on the news. This cousin lives about an hour west of Denver. She had another good visit from Helen whom some of us had visited earlier.

January 15 if anything family was done, it had to be me doing it. Ruth had some difficulty ordering from the menu, so I ordered for her. That evening I ordered pot roast (shredded beef style), cooked carrots, chocolate pudding, and grape nectar. She fed herself with no problem. She didn't really like the thick grape nectar, but she devoured the rest. I had to smile at her style: She mixed the cooked carrots in with the pot roast and ate it all together. If she liked it that way, why not?

I complimented her for eating her chocolate pudding so well. She said, "That's like complimenting a child for eating his ice cream." So what if it was! She was doing well, and I intended to cheer her along all the way.

January 16 was to be our last full day in Denver. We were excited about that, but not everything was as it should be. Ruth seemed to be quite confused, and I had questions I was not getting answered.

A sign on the back of Ruth's wheel chair read "acute therapy." She read that and was sure it was related somehow to chocolate pancakes. And those chocolate pancakes were somehow also related to McDonalds.

But Pastor Tom came to visit. He suggested we say Psalm 23 together. We did, and Ruth said it all word for word. Her mind seemed clearest when speaking of Scripture or of spiritual matters.

And my questions? I could hardly believe my eyes! About noon I happened to go to the nurses' station, and there were

Dr. Elliot, our lead doctor, Dr. Bellon, our coiling specialist, and Tyler, our favorite physicians' assistant. My questions were answered then and again later in the evening when I again saw Tyler. And, yes, Ruth would be leaving in the morning for Montana!

Our children understandably had some concerns and asked me to try to get answers. The first was about Ruth's blood pressure—it was higher than in the past. Would it continue that way? The answer was that they were not sure. She might need to be on some medication the rest of her life to manage it.

The second was the effects of many medications she had taken while there. They said it was possible that her emotions could be flatter than they had been in the past. I wrote in an email to the children: "But she and I had a great talk yesterday before the crew from Glendive arrived and after; she did show some emotion. It'll be good, even if it is not exactly the same."

The third question concerned the heredity of aneurysms. The answer surprised me. They are not hereditary unless there is a history of kidney problems in the family. (Later we discussed the subject with another physician at home, and the answer was the same. Perhaps there is not a direct connection between the two, but there has been an observed tendency toward aneurysms when certain kidney problems exist in a particular family.) To our knowledge there was no history of kidney problems in our families.

Arlie and Ruth, 40th Anniversary Alaska Cruise, June 26, 2011

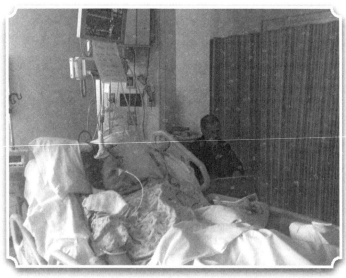

Ruth in Swedish Hospital's Critical Care
Unit after ventilator was removed

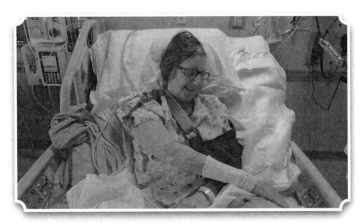

Ruth in Neuro Unit with NG removed

Arlie and Merrily taking Ruth for a wheelchair ride

Ruth beginning to eat thickened liquids

Ruth at New Hope in Billings for rehab

Renessa helping Ruth walk with the walker

Leaving New Hope for home in Glendive

Ruth at Community Bible Church walking with a cane

Family at Lake Tahoe, CA, reunion July of 2013
Back row: Christy holding Levi, Carmody, Renessa holding
Maisie, Sy, Andrae, Monica, Merrily, Hans
Front row: Ella, Alethia, Winslow, Arlie
and Ruth, Josiah, Ethan

CHAPTER 9

THE OTHER SIDE OF
STAGE THREE (PART 1)

It is comfortable to have our own children here. And that is a double blessing when they, too, are part of the Body of Christ. We have such precious times together discussing everything under the sun and expressing a wide range of emotions together freely.

"Behold, children are a gift of the LORD; the fruit of the womb is a reward.

Like arrows in the hands of a warrior, So are the children of one's youth.

How blessed is the man whose quiver is full of them." (Ps. 127:3-5)

"Her children rise up and bless her." (Prov. 31:28a)

But now I must report on my (Ruth's, too, of course, but this for now only impacts me) unruly children. They have been involved in some questionable activities. In fact, they have been plotting behind my back.

Even further, the other evening Merrily and I were ready to leave the hospital and return to our temporary home, and Hans calmly ignored us, talking on his iPhone for another half hour! What should be done with kids like this?

I discovered later that when we were waiting for him, he was talking with Andrae in California, Carmody in Arizona, and Sy on the other side of the world, all at the same time. And do you know what they were discussing? They were discussing finances. What they were really discussing was a system by which they could handle the financial side of this adventure without me having to be involved in it. They want me to focus on caring for Ruth and the ministry God has given me.

I have occasionally thought about the cost of all this. It'll be fun to see the actual number. I laugh when I think about it, because I'm sure I could sell all I have and not pay for it. But God owns the cattle on a thousand hills, and I fully expect that all the bills will be paid.

We do belong to Samaritan Ministries, and this will be another way that the Body of Christ shares. But my kids have already been in contact with Samaritan Ministries, and they are planning to handle everything.

So, what do you do with kids like that? I told them I'd get even, and I am as I write this. I guess I'll keep them, love them even more, and be as proud of them as I can! Is that ok? (They'll be embarrassed if they knew I had written this, so don't tell them about it.)

from the Care Page

People continued to show God's love to us. On January 6 Dave came from Colorado Springs with soup and bread. It was delicious!

A few days later a box came from Andrae and Monica. It was full of treats that I enjoy. These were very useful, especially later as I traveled. I commented over the phone to Andrae that it appeared Monica had had a hand in this. His reply? "She had both hands in it." It was a box full of love.

We continued to attend Hillcrest Christian Reformed Church as long as we were in Denver. The pastor and people were welcoming. The songs were wonderful. January 8 the message was "Seven Things About Heaven" out of Revelation 21. It was nourishing to our souls.

Since I am a pastor, I am usually concerned with the mechanics of a church service. "Mechanics"—what a strange word in such a setting. Yet one needs to have some sense of order, sequence, and timing. Occasionally it is therapeutic to sit in someone else's service and just soak in everything. I found that in this time of suffering I was very sensitive. I went to the services there hungry, and my soul feasted on each part of the meeting. The songs overwhelmed me, but I sang as I could.

With Ruth's move from critical care to a different floor for recovery, my life was filled with calls and visits about future care and about financial matters. Some of this was distasteful as it seemed crass to me to frame the discussion about Ruth's recovery in terms of how much money we were willing to spend.

Merrily and I had one such visit with the social worker, and I decided I needed to direct the conversation. After her introduction with money seeming to be the critical factor, I demanded of her that we discuss this without talk of money. Once we focused on rehabilitation options alone, we did have a profitable session.

My sensitivity extended far beyond only the church services. I was strengthened by people who simply smiled at me. I wrote the following in the Care Page for January 11:

> A theme that has been on my mind is the power of a smile. Proverbs 15:13 says, "A joyful heart makes a cheerful face, But when the

heart is sad, the spirit is broken." I have seen both in the last few weeks. But I so appreciate a smile. And many folks have blessed me with one. And I think that in itself has encouraged me not to take people for granted. A lady on a bicycle today smiled at me. I have never seen her before and probably never will again, but I was encouraged.

Tyler, one of our [lead] doctor's assistants, we love. He is so good at communicating the medical details of Ruth's condition. He is always calm and has a wonderful smile. Of course, it did not hurt one bit today when he said that what is happening inside Ruth's brain is ahead of schedule. In fact, he said that for her injury with its level of severity and the time involved this was the best result he had ever seen. Praise God! He is answering prayers. We don't always see progress from one day to the next, but inside there is progress—ahead of schedule!

On this floor, floor seven, there is a young man who empties the trash. He has a nice smile. I like to chat with him. He has a never ending job, but he doesn't complain. Oh, I'm sure he gets paid for it, but his smile encourages us.

Ruth's speech therapist has a great smile. She
reminds me of someone, I think from back
home, but I can't think yet of who it is. She
just beams when she is here, and sometimes
we, including Ruth, laugh with her.

In addition to spending time with Ruth, there were normal
details of life that continued to require my attention. Folks
back home were sending me our mail, and they also sent the
estimated payment forms for state and federal income taxes.
These needed to be paid even though life was abnormal. I
was able to pay those on time, and I continued to be grateful
for the church folks back home who were making it possible
for me to take care of those items.

Sometimes you know in your mind how something should
work, but others make it difficult. A patient advocate kept
calling to talk with me. With her concern, she needed to
talk to Hans, not me. But she would only talk to me. She
would call when I was not available. So I would call back,
and she would not be in. Finally through some round-a-
bout channels we were able to get someone with authority
to communicate to her that it was ok to talk to Hans.

Some years ago I had read "A Shepherd Looks at Psalm
23" by Philip Keller. Otis had loaned me the book, so I
finally managed reading it again. I was sensitive to this
book as well. The circumstances allowed for it to speak to
our situation. In the Care Page for January 13 I wrote this:

> … the sheep who has a good shepherd does
> not try to step away from the relationship
> with that shepherd. That sheep is content
> and will always be content in the shepherd's
> presence. Life does sometimes tear my
> insides out, but I am content with my
> Shepherd.

And I was content with the Lord Jesus who is the Good Shepherd.

I thought about theological subjects that now became experience. The Body of Christ had surrounded us with love. It was fascinating to me to note that God in His sovereign care does not permit all in the Body of Christ to be equally afflicted simultaneously. Those who are not afflicted currently can minister to those who are. We knew of several other people suffering at the same time we were, but there existed for each a constituency of support and encouragement.

I also wondered about Satan's part in all this. I wrote again January 14:

> I haven't been shown Satan's part in all
> this. We do know that God initiated the
> situation in which Satan afflicted Job (Job
> 1:8) by divine permission. But Satan is on a
> leash. He can only go so far (Job 1:12; 2:6).

And so we can say with Joseph to Satan or maybe even to others in some cases, You meant it for evil, but God meant it for good (Gen. 50:20).

It is an unparalleled good to be a conduit for the love of God. Has Ruth suffered? Yes, and she has a long road back. Again, in the mercy of God, she doesn't remember the worst of it. She only remembers the irritations of recovery.

Have I suffered? Yes, like never before. I experienced it all. Am I angry at God? No, not at all. I remember when I first found Ruth; immediately I knew that our only hope was in God, no matter what shape this would take. One of the possible outcomes was devastating to me, but I always knew God was my only hope.

I haven't had to pay the ultimate price. Jesus did. There is no way I can fault Him for His work in my life when He has loved me so much as to lay down His life for me (John 10: 11, 15, 17-18). But what a blessing it is that when Jesus laid down His life He had power to take it up again! He is our hope!

And then Romans 8:28 promises that all things work together for good to those who love God. You probably cannot believe the good we have seen already! And it is likely that we have seen only a small part of the good He is doing through this. I'm not being cynical here; I wish like everything that Ruth had not had to suffer. But we will agree with Job's words in 23:10: "But He knows the way I take; When He has tried me, I shall come forth as gold." Job wrote that in the context of not quite understanding what God was doing, and we agree in the same spirit.

Some days later I returned to third floor to deliver a 'thank you' card to the nursing staff there. I hadn't paid much attention when we moved from third to seventh floor, but when I went back I noticed a huge difference.

There was the question of life and death on floor three. On floor seven the problems had been fixed; now the goal was to get the body to regain its original functions. It was a time for recovery. The atmosphere was different.

Not only that. The critical care room had seemed small and packed with equipment. The floor seven rooms were almost like suites. The rooms were three times as large with windows and sofas; we could see the snow-capped mountains from there. The machinery was minimal. Instead therapists came and went.

Sometimes I met people we first came to know in the critical care waiting room. One day some from the family whose son and brother had been in a bad car accident happened to be walking the same direction in a hall at the same time we were. So I chatted with the mother. She had some good news, and I had some good news. We loved to share good news!

People were being checked into the critical care unit every day. New people arrived with new tears. We heard of an accident involving college students from Kansas. One was paralyzed. We live in a world where anything can go wrong, and it sometimes does. No one is exempt from that. Are you prepared for the worst?

I cried often, sometimes out of grief, sometimes out of joy. Others who may have observed perhaps could not tell the difference. There was suffering, but there was also joy in the suffering because of the love of God and the kindness of others.

One of the themes Ruth emphasized in raising our children is that they would learn to be kind. It was a special blessing to realize the kindness of others to me. It was exhibited by people who knew us, but often as well by complete strangers. It eased the pain of suffering and surely was a gift from God.

CHAPTER 10

THE OTHER SIDE OF STAGE THREE (PART 2)

I thought I would have lots of time to read while here, but it is difficult to find the time. Don't ask me what we do all day—it's difficult to explain. Mail from home has been sent to me; I have been able to take care of the usual bills, and we have read most of the Christmas letters, etc., but the magazines are piling up.

Just today, however, I finished reading "A Shepherd Looks at Psalm 23" after not having touched it for a long time. This is a book I read years ago, but this time it really spoke to my situation. The last part of the psalm says, "And I will dwell in the house of the LORD forever." We could quibble about the translation from the Hebrew, but we must interpret from the perspective of the sheep. Baaaa.

The point of that is that the sheep who has a good shepherd does not try to step away from the relationship with that shepherd. That sheep is content and will always be content in the shepherd's presence. Life does sometimes tear my insides out, but I am content with my Shepherd. If you want to know about my Good Shepherd, read the Bible, John 10.

from the Care Page

The evening of January 6 is stuck in my memory. I was in my bedroom at my temporary 'home' in Denver sobbing my way though Psalm 34. I can't tell you why I chose Psalm 34, but Ruth and I had chosen verse three for our wedding verse, and so the pastor used it in his message over forty years ago. It says, "O magnify the LORD with me, And let us exalt His name together."

As I read through the psalm, it seemed as though the entire psalm had been written for me. Or even as though I had written all of it out of this experience. And the verse that summed up all for me was verse six, "This poor man cried and the LORD heard him, And saved him out of all his troubles." I realized that I was poor in every way you might consider, I had cried out to the LORD and continued doing so, and the LORD did hear me.

Later I reflected on that experience. Why did my emotions spill out over that psalm? And the answer came as I went back and researched what had happened leading up to that evening. There were powerful reasons.

Three days before I had been discouraged over Ruth's progress. We were told during the morning conference that her heart was misbehaving some. Also, her lungs had unwanted fluid in them. Some of her numbers were good, but the complications weighed on me. These conditions existed at least partly due to her being bedridden for so long; they were not directly caused by the brain injury.

I wrote the following to someone in an email that day:

> The Body of Christ has been amazing. I am
> discouraged at times, but it's not because of
> other people—thousands are praying and
> extending help. Your prayers are the most
> helpful!

It was true that people were very encouraging. When I was discouraged, I did not attribute the cause to other Christians nor to God. It was my own problem, my weakness of faith.

In another email I wrote:

> Everyone is so good to me. If I have down
> days, it's not their fault. I find that the only
> thing strong about my faith is Jesus, whom

I trust. I am so weak. But He has carried
me when I had nothing on which to go.

Two days before January 6 I did not go to the hospital. I
was sick. It seemed like a digestive ailment was making its
rounds and finally, combined with stress, it took me down.
I was content to stay in bed most of the day. It would have
been easy to blame it on the meatloaf I had with our friend
who took us out to eat, but I don't think that was in any way
related to the problem!

The day spent at home was not wasted; I was involved in a
significant amount of phone conversations interspersed with
sleep. And the next day I did feel somewhat better, so much
better in fact that I resumed hospital visitation. But food was
still not attractive to me.

Actually, January 4, the day I stayed in bed, was a very
good day in other respects. Ruth was moved out of the
Critical Care Unit on third floor and transferred to the
Neurosciences Nursing Unit on the seventh floor. That was
welcome news even though I was not there to participate
in it. And I did wonder at the time whether she had been
moved too soon. Apparently they even had her in a chair for
a while. All this was cause for great rejoicing!

The day before my Psalm 34 experience a sharply dressed
gentleman entered Ruth's room, told us bluntly what our
costs at Swedish Medical Center were projected to be, and

said that payment would be due in two days. Now I was not surprised at the figures—numbers have always been fun for me even when figuring income tax! But I could not appreciate the man's (or hospital's) method and policy.

It later became clear with further exchange that he was saying the payment would be due not two days from January 5, but two days after Ruth's discharge. He also indicated there would be a significant discount since we were not insured.

I could possibly have assembled the funds to pay this bill, but it was impossible that I could do so without being home. Furthermore, even if I were home, the process would take longer than two days.

I was definitely shocked by the man's sudden appearance and mission. In my naive way of thinking, I could conceive of the interested parties at some point inviting me into a conference room or office to discuss the financial arrangements. This was certainly a low point in what was otherwise a professional and humane delivery of medical care.

The impact of that visit may have stayed with me longer, but a couple hours later I discovered that Hans in Minnesota and Andrae in California were already aware of these charges and were in contact with people who were likely the superiors of the man who visited Ruth's room. Our sons were already on the case! This was one of many times their activity on our behalf was a comfort.

Finally on the very day of my Psalm 34 experience, I awoke feeling physically much better. As became my habit, I listened to our local radio station back home, KGLE at AM 590, via computer streaming. I was blessed to hear the Haven Quartet sing "It Won't Be Long." There is nothing like suffering that moves me to look toward heaven.

That morning Ruth's feeding tube was not working properly. Most of us visiting had not worked with hospital equipment, but it was obvious to us where the problem was. The bottle with its solution was fine. But the tube had air pockets in it, and that was not good. The problem had to be in the connection where the bottle and tube met.

The nurse that day could not solve the problem. She began replacing parts. And no doubt every part was another charge on our bill. But her replacements did nothing to correct the problem.

Now Carmody's wife, Christy, is an ICU nurse and actually teaches other ICU nurses. So once when that day's nurse was out of the room, Christy dissembled the unit, corrected the tab that was not properly open, and the problem was gone. Her fix only required a few seconds. When the nurse returned, she became angry when Christy informed her of the repair. Christy didn't work there and was not to be involving herself! But, from our view, it had to be done, the nurse was not getting it done, and Christy had solved the problem! Christy's presence at that time was another evidence of God's care for us.

So, why did I sob through my extended reading of Psalm 34? Maybe it was because of the physical challenges of being fatigued and sick. Maybe it was because of the joy of Ruth's transition out of the Critical Care Unit and the surrounding help of others. Maybe it was because of the emotional exhaustion of those days. Maybe it was all of those possibilities converging at once. But I was grateful to God for His daily provision for this poor man.

CHAPTER 11

STAGE FOUR—ACUTE REHAB AT NEW HOPE (PART 1)

Transition

Ruth's doctors had at some point suggested that we might travel to Billings by car for acute rehab. It seemed incredible to me that Ruth would be able to travel that way, and I was not sure I could handle it. One problem was that I did not have our car in Denver. So we researched the various possibilities.

Our church leaders back home formed an excellent plan. Don and Deb had just purchased a Chevrolet Suburban that would work comfortably for this trip. Ruth could even lie down if necessary. Good friends, Otis and Miriam, were available during that time to come to Denver with the Suburban and a nurse. So they arrived the evening of January 16. I joined them that night at the Marriott so we could leave together in the morning.

We had first planned on leaving by 5 or 6 AM; if we could arrive in Billings by afternoon some introductions could be done yet that day. The trip was slightly over 550 miles, all of it interstate; we were looking at about an eight-hour trip. But we couldn't leave as early as we had wanted. Physical therapists were needed to load Ruth into the Suburban; they did not work night shifts, and they arrived for work at 7 AM. And we had discharge papers to sign. So we began loading after 7 AM. Three therapists were required to help Ruth into the Suburban because she was still quite helpless. At this point it was a challenge for her even to sit up.

So we actually drove away from the hospital about 8 AM, and it took another hour before the city limits of Denver were finally behind us. We were on our way to Montana—not quite home yet, but a big step in the right direction.

We had been acquainted with Carolyn, our nurse, but we didn't know her well. During the trip we came to appreciate her very much. She is older than we are, but you would never have known it. When I offered to tilt the second row seat so she could get into the back of the Suburban where she would ride, she declined, and proceeded to just climb over.

She took total care of Ruth. She watched over her with full attention. We couldn't have known what care Ruth would need on the way, but having Carolyn along put us at ease. She was well familiar with Ruth's accompanying equipment. And she was a lively part of the conversation as well.

We are not sure how Ruth sat up all the way to Billings, but she did. She seemed to improve some that day. She talked much, and her volume increased. We concluded that she felt she had to speak louder in order to offset road noise. Some of her conversation was about significant, abstract issues. She also showed more ability to move her left leg.

She was sitting on a pad in the Suburban, and it somehow bothered her. So she tried to pull it out. We tried to talk her out of that attempt, but our efforts were in vain. Fortunately, she did not succeed. Also, when we stopped various times, she was determined to jump out! The most she managed was to undo her seat belt a few times.

All in all it was a good trip. Of course, being January, it was cold, but it was also a beautiful day, with mostly clear skies. Passing through Wyoming we encountered strong winds, but since the roads were clear, it was not a problem. There was a bit of drifting snow occasionally. We didn't stop except briefly for gas, comfort, and some food. Ruth said once that it was a crazy day; we concluded it was because of who all were in the car!

We did not arrive at New Hope in Billings early enough to discuss therapy that day. But they were ready for us. So by supper time Tuesday, January 17, Ruth had been settled into her new home at the New Hope acute rehabilitation center in St. Vincent Healthcare, room #458. The fourth floor is the patient floor, and the fifth floor is the therapy center with many different kinds of exercise equipment.

Being here was much different than the other stages of hospital stay. Perhaps I could describe it by saying that the patients in rehab were not so much ill or injured. That had been corrected, but now they needed to learn the motions of living again and perhaps to compensate for their handicaps. One of the significant benefits of having moved to acute rehab was that now Ruth could wear her normal clothes. We were all happy to say 'good-by' to the hospital gown. She joined the others who were there looking more normal. It was almost like a school rather than a hospital.

Don and Deb had brought my car to Billings, so I now had transportation. The first few nights I stayed at Hilltop Inn which is very close to New Hope. I only had to walk one block outside and then I could walk the sky bridges to cross over into the hospital. Some days I was able to spend as much as eleven hours with Ruth during this time. During her entire stay there my plan was to eat the evening meal with her in the Diner's Club where she ate. I could order a tasty and nutritious meal at a very reasonable price from the cafeteria, and it would be served along with hers.

We ate with other patients in the Diner's Club and enjoyed interaction with them; some were in rehab because of strokes or various accidents. As we became acquainted, we would share our stories. We all cheered when someone reached a milestone or was ready to be discharged.

I was hoping to find a home where I could stay nights and which would have space for me to set up my desktop computer so I could study. I had several offers, and the one that I accepted was David's uncle and aunt, Dave and Kay; David is part of our church. I had not known them previously, but I came to appreciate them much. They are another of God's significant couples here on earth! Dave and I would visit before I left to see Ruth almost each day, and the visiting was so enjoyable that I usually left later than I had planned. So after that first partial week I stayed with them.

Therapy

There were two reasons why Ruth was without so much bodily function and needed therapy. First, the ruptured brain aneurysm had effectively shut down the brain's communication to various part of the body. Second was the month on her back. The lack of activity combined with the brain bleed had been quite effective in taking away her past abilities.

Our first full day in Billings, January 18, a team of six met with Ruth and me to discuss their plan. Essentially their goal was to prepare Ruth to go home. That sounded good to me! It would take physical, occupational, speech, and recreational therapies to accomplish this. I personally came to believe that we had some of the best therapists anywhere. They understood Ruth's abilities or lack of them and knew exactly what to do to help her safely. I was usually there for therapy, so we all became good friends.

When we were still in Denver we were told that Ruth would likely be in therapy three months, maybe even four or five. However, the staff at New Hope projected that Ruth might reach the goals they had set within four to six weeks. That was good to hear, but I thought it was optimistic.

Diane, the physical therapist, worked with such things as strength and motor deficits, balance, help for basic tasks such as getting out of bed. Erica, the occupational therapist, worked with the activities of daily living, such as taking care of oneself, bathroom visits, bathing, getting a drink of water, etc.

Kyle, the speech therapist, worked with swallowing so Ruth's eating and drinking could return to normal, with cognitive skills to recall issues, and with attentional ability. All three of these therapies we would need to continue after leaving New Hope.

Rosanna, the recreational therapist, worked in the area of activities Ruth might enjoy doing; it would involve mobility skills, safety in recreation, fall prevention, and energy conservation.

Shawna, the nurse and the fifth person on the team, let us know that she would be monitoring tube feedings, bowel and bladder control, medication, incision care, and stroke education.

Finally Mary, the social worker and sixth team member, said she would help us with planning so that eventually Ruth would have a smooth transition to home.

That first day Ruth had the full range of therapies. The most exciting outcome of that first day was that she was taken off of thick liquids and now free to eat and drink anything. She had convinced the speech therapist that she could do it, and she could! She needed to take small sips and then think 'swallow quickly.' That worked well for her. We also learned that hotter or colder liquids are more effective in stimulating the epiglottis to move quickly.

In speech therapy she had to switch back and forth between naming opposites and doing math problems. I thought she did well even though after ten minutes or so her attention would wane. But she still could not understand why she could not just get up and go do anything she wished. Yet in the dining room, seeing others in similar condition, she commented that some of them had no one to love them. She sometimes asked me for a kiss, and I happily supplied her request!

Visitors

We had thought that once we were back in Montana Ruth would receive visitors from home (even though home was 220 miles from Billings), and that would help her to reorient herself. We thought correctly. Hardly a day went by without company. A couple of families came to visit. Numerous couples came. And a number of individuals.

Some were from our church in Glendive, and some were from entirely different communities. Those from elsewhere were surprises, but their interest was a special treat. A few were relatives. Some we really did not know very well, but, again, their compassion in coming was encouraging.

One surprise to us was that most of those who visited stayed a long time. It was common to visit two hours. We valued their investment of time in us. It enabled us to actually share our experience and theirs and to catch up on news. Every visitor strengthened us by their presence and their interest. Each was part of God's love to us.

Their time spent with us was beyond value. We think back fondly to those times spent in conversation.

We also received lots of phone calls. Most of these were from family members, but some were from others.

The First Memory

January 20 is the first day Ruth remembers. She remembers it because of what happened. She was sitting in her room in the wheel chair. I decided to leave for a few minutes to get some coffee from the Bistro. So I informed a recreational therapist who was at the nurse's station and left.

When I returned the door to Ruth's room was shut. I knocked and then pushed it slowly open. Ruth was lying on the floor. At first I was somewhat peeved at the therapist who said they would look after her. I later learned that she had informed the other nurses, but what happened happened in a moment of time—they simply could not prevent it.

Ruth had decided to get up and go. Of course, she really couldn't, so she just fell down. Then she saw that the door was open and she could be seen. So she pushed the door shut. After that they realized how closely she needed to be watched. Fortunately she was not injured. She simply did not understand that she could not walk.

I was told that patients with injury on the right side of the brain, such as Ruth had, tended to be impulsive and would try to get up and walk. They are at risk of falling. To mark her as a fall risk, she had a yellow sock on her door and a yellow blanket in her room.

After One Week

When we arrived in Billings, there was little normal that Ruth could do. She had just gained enough strength and balance to be able to sit up without support. She could not stand or walk. Her right hand was strong, but her left was not. She could move her legs some, but her left leg was very sluggish. She was just learning to swallow and talk out loud again.

We had been told by the therapists that progress might be slow. They warned us not to measure her progress day by day, but rather week by week. Some days her abilities might even regress. We were fortunate in that we were able to see some progress almost every day. Sometimes it was very small, but we celebrated every success. I appointed myself as her number one cheerleader!

After we had been at New Hope for one week, the difference was tremendous! Now Ruth could easily sit up. One day she had her right leg drawn up with her right knee pointing at the ceiling. Suddenly she pulled the left one up right beside it. She had not yet done that for the therapist. It seemed like sometimes she couldn't do what the therapist asked, though she tried. At other times she did it on her own, as though she was thinking, "What's the big deal? I used to do this all the time!"

Her usual way of getting around was in the wheel chair at this point. She had some difficulty coordinating her limbs so that it would go straight. But the physical therapist was not content with her managing the wheel chair. She could get herself out of the wheel chair and onto another surface. She was also walking now between the parallel bars. She could walk the twenty feet, turn around, and come back. She looked very good being upright after so long on her back. She had lost some weight, but she was concerned that she was eating too much!

A few days before she had trouble when we took her to the piano and gave her a hymnal. She could play the right hand just fine, but the left hand could not accurately play the bass. She was usually a note off. But now she did play again! She played well with both hands, and began to pedal with the right foot as well. The first time I heard it, it was so beautiful to me that I had to walk away and cry. We eventually recorded her playing "What a Friend We Have in Jesus" and posted it on YouTube. People across the country and even beyond heard her play and with tears of joy joined us in praise to the Lord who had given back that ability. She did lots of piano playing for one of the recreational therapists and also read background stories of hymns to her.

Speech therapy probably intrigued me the most. I was glad I didn't have to take the tests Ruth had! Clock exercises that had been difficult at first were improving. Sometimes she was given various kinds of paperwork, and then she would be interrupted with math questions. Could she handle the concentration and distractions? She usually did well at first, but after about ten minutes her attention would wane.

One day the speech therapist gave her a grid with letters on it. She should construct words using adjacent letters in any direction. That might have been fun, but as she did that he would read to her. Then later he asked her questions about the reading. Or he would give her a sequence of numbers. After engaging her in other activities, he would ask her to repeat the number sequence. She did amazingly well. Her cognitive abilities were returning rapidly.

Ruth continued to be confused about time. I was not surprised by that on the one hand, because a whole month was missing from her memory. To her the number "12" did not seem like it could designate a year. And after an afternoon nap, she would think it was time for breakfast when in fact it was time for supper. I would clarify the situation for her, and she accepted it. She somehow knew that she was confused. And then the next day I would have to give the explanation again.

She was becoming more curious about what had happened. She wanted to know the details. The actual understanding and acceptance of the facts took some time, but eventually she was amazed at all that had happened, about her time in Denver, and about the trip to Billings.

In some ways she was definitely herself. One day in speech therapy she said she wanted to serve some food to the 'men.' The men were the speech therapist and me! Actually she did later have that opportunity.

She was also now eating and drinking any kinds of food and drink she wished. She was able to order off a menu, and the food was quite good. Her intake of food was observed closely to make sure that she received the nutrition she needed. She was also free of all tubes except her PEG. And that could still be used for extra nutrition or medication if necessary.

One day that week she asked suddenly where her rings were. The rings were removed early in this saga, but one would not come off. I even gave permission to have it cut off if necessary. But a nurse in Denver said she was good at removing rings, and she did manage to get it off. It was important to remove the rings because of all the fluids they had to pump into her. By this time the swelling from all that fluid was long gone.

I had kept the rings in a safe place, and I was happy to report the same to her. After more than a month she had noticed their absence! We did joke on that occasion that at least she knew she was married to me even though she didn't have rings on her fingers. Actually, maybe that wasn't a joking matter, because some have awakened after such an injury and no longer knew who they were.

I made a quick trip home the first Saturday to get necessary items. But I also brought back two Christmas presents—one for her and one for me. You see, we had not celebrated our Christmas yet. The two presents I brought back were both books: a hymn book which included the hymn's background stories for Ruth, and for me a history of the Bible focusing on themes such as assembly of the books of the Bible, translations, and challenges from the beginning until now.

I continued to write almost daily for Ruth's Care Page. That weekend she posted for her Care Page. Actually she wrote the message out long hand, and I then entered it into the computer. Many people responded to my posts on the Care Page, but when she wrote the responses increased greatly. It was good for folks to hear directly from her.

The therapists asked for information about conditions at home. Some modifications were needed especially for bathroom activities. We were open to anything we would need to do, but in the end the only significant changes were some grab rails in the bathroom, a tub bench, and a hand-held shower. Some men from the church would be happy to install whatever we needed.

My daily one-minute radio program was airing even while I was away. But I needed to continue to produce. I had recorded some programs via cell phone when I was in Denver, and now I recorded some on a digital recorder. I did it in perhaps the quietest place I could find—my car. But it worked fairly well and kept the program going.

CHAPTER 12

THE OTHER SIDE OF STAGE FOUR

I spent a long time looking at Psalm 49 before I went to bed last night. I had planned to preach on that psalm the first two Sundays of the new year. It's noteworthy that in the critical care waiting room we do not visit with others about how much money they are making.

Instead we ask, How is your loved one doing? Everything is a matter of life and death and relationship, and that really helps to focus your attention on the text of Scripture, because there it is, also. No matter how much of this world's goods one has, or how much insurance one has, you cannot redeem someone's life from the grave. But God is the great Redeemer; He can redeem someone's life from the grave, and so our faith rests in Him according to the Scriptures.

It's been about ten days since we moved from critical care on the third floor to the neuro unit on seventh floor. I went back the other day to deliver a 'thank you' card. What a difference between the two floors! I had not considered that until I went back. May I say that I am glad we are on the seventh floor.

Sometimes I meet people we first met in the critical care waiting room. I did again yesterday. I met the Mexican family whose son and brother was in a bad car accident. We happened to be going the same direction down the hall. So I chatted with the mother. She had some good news, and I had some good news.

from the Care Page

I was welcome to be with Ruth all day if I wished. Therapy, which I could attend, began in the morning and usually was done by 3 PM. We encouraged visitors to come after that.

That first part of a week in Billings I went to New Hope early and stayed until about 8 PM. But my schedule changed the second week. On Saturday, January 21, I made a quick trip home 220 miles one way to get various supplies. I was at home only about two hours. The trip seemed strange. Glendive was home and had been for over twenty-one years, and yet I returned as a visitor.

Most important among the supplies I brought back was my desktop computer so I could study in Billings. My plan was to go home Saturdays beginning January 28, preach

Sundays at Community Bible Church, and then return. So at that point I devoted mornings to Bible study at my 'home' in Billings and arrived at New Hope closer to noon. I spent the rest of the day with Ruth. I would tell her my schedule the day before, and yet frequently when I arrived she would say with a smile, "I'm surprised to see you."

The next two weekends I returned to Glendive Saturday to a whirlwind of activities, preached Sunday morning, and then returned to Billings. I was actually somewhat concerned about my first time back. But the Lord was preparing my way. I first stopped at a hardware store when I got back, and there was Paul, a gentleman from church. We hugged and talked. Then that evening I was invited to the home of a couple from church, Keith and Jeanne, for supper. The couple of hours that we ate and talked eased me back into the home church setting.

It was still challenging to preach those Sundays, and yet it was good. Singing was especially difficult for me. I felt a greater need than usual for the Lord's strength, and He gave it. The folks at church gave me lots of hugs and many good wishes for Ruth.

January 29 the community's churches held a regular fifth-Sunday-of-the-month singspiration. We would normally have been a part of it, but obviously this time we were absent. This one was different in that it was designated as a fund raiser for Ruth. Apparently the turnout was good, and we were astounded at the generosity of those who attended. It was a blessing to us, since in such times money comes and goes, and you cannot always think through what is the most frugal. Again we saw God blessing us through other people.

I continued during that time to think through our experience in relation to Scripture. My adult life had been involved in study of the Bible, so this was only natural. Now I was experiencing personally what in some cases I could before proclaim truthfully—because God's word is truth—and yet without experience. There was a new dimension in my meditation. The following are various subjects I considered and shared with others via the Care Page.

In university days a medical doctor told me that I was a very tense person. I will not try to diagnose the cause of that, but for a while I purposely focused on Scriptures that tell us to rest. For example, Psalm 91:14-16 says: "Because he has loved Me, therefore I will deliver him; I will set him securely on high, because he has known My name. He will call upon Me, and I will answer him; I will be with him in trouble; I will rescue him, and honor him. With a long life I will satisfy him, And let him behold My salvation."

Sometimes in search for a particular theme I ran across some other treat. In that passage I was impressed that the LORD put emphasis on someone loving Him. All the promises stated there are based upon someone loving God. But I also remembered that 1 John 4 in that long essay on love tells us that love comes from God and we love because He first loved us. On the Care Page I wrote this:

> The humbling beauty in this is that God treats our love of Him as though it is something special when He Himself gave us that love in the first place. But that's what God is like. Why would someone not want to know a God like that?

Another day I was still researching rest. That day the passage was Psalm 116:7: "Return to your rest, O my soul, For the LORD has dealt bountifully with you." I could rest as I considered the goodness of God to me. It may seem odd to revel in the goodness of God during a time of suffering, but I did.

Verse 13 in the same psalm says, "I shall lift up the cup of salvation, And call upon the name of the LORD." The mention of salvation there reminded me that in this whole experience I have especially been comforted by the Scriptures that speak of Christ's salvation worked on the cross for us. I think that is because my real need is not for someone to hold my hand, but it is for Someone to tell me that my sin-debt has been paid and I am eternally safe in the Savior. All of life can fall apart, and in many ways it has, but this is what counts.

January 21 on my trip back to Glendive I was meditating on love. One of my thoughts was the difficulty of evaluating one's own love. Jeremiah 17:9 tells us our hearts are tricky, and 1 John 3:20 suggests that our hearts might even sometime wrongly condemn us, but God is also aware of that. It is best to trust God's word over against our own feelings. So I wrote in the Care Page:

> Maybe that is why love is defined in the Bible in objective terms in 1 John 5:2-3: "By this we know that we love the children of God, when we love God and observe His commandments. For this is the love of God, that we keep His commandments." So if we are keeping God's commands, we are loving.

> But on the other hand, it is easy to observe when others love me. It is obvious when I am on the receiving end. And our local church surely has loved us. It has expressed itself in giving time, energy, and resources, some directly to us and some in taking care of responsibilities we would normally have. We would like to pay them back, but it is impossible. Furthermore, they understand that as they love us.

Sometimes when hospital officials learn about what our church is doing for us, they say, "It looks like you have a good support group in place." It's that, and more. As someone said at the hospital in Glendive on December 19, "We're family." Make that God's family.

Ruth and I both miss the fellowship of our local church, and we will be back as soon as possible—I sooner and she later, Lord willing.

Another day I was thinking about the biblical prophets and how God sometimes used them and their families as object lessons. Ezekiel was one of those. In chapter 24 God told him his wife would die and he was not to mourn her death openly. That might be difficult for most, but it would be especially difficult in that culture where there was a pronounced emphasis on the display of mourning. Of course, his role had prophetic significance for the message he was announcing to the people of Judah who were in captivity in Babylon.

There are actually people who do not grieve at the death of a spouse. Sometimes they have suffered so much because of that spouse while living that there is no more grief to express. That death may even be a sort of relief. This was not the case for Ezekiel whose wife is described as "the desire of his eyes." He obviously loved her dearly.

I have thought that what God asked of Ezekiel was difficult. Maybe I could even commiserate with him a bit now. To lose her was bad enough. But not to mourn her death? To keep the grief bottled up inside? Yet all that was in service to a loving God who had to send a difficult message to His unbelieving people.

Then I saw again the great mercy God had poured out upon me. He had not asked anything that difficult of me. I added in the Care Page:

> Sheldon Vanauken enjoyed an idyllic marriage with his wife. When she died fairly young, C. S. Lewis, a friend, wrote him to tell him essentially (I'm not quoting here) that her death was an extreme mercy to him so that he might love God with all his heart instead of his love for her being supreme. A husband is to love his wife as Christ loved the Church, but can a husband love his wife more than he loves Christ? We are to love God with our whole heart, soul, strength, and mind. He is to be supreme.

I was thinking early one morning again about the cleaning lady in Denver who prayed for Ruth every day when she came into the room and who said that our room was full of love. Her presence, service, and words greatly encouraged us! What was different in our room than in other rooms? I could not put myself into her shoes and experience what she did in all the rooms she entered. I don't remember doing anything 'religious' while she was there.

But then I read in Matthew 6 that Jesus instructs us not to be showy in the expression of our relationship to Him. This contrasts those who wear certain clothes as though to impress us with their 'holiness.' I concluded again that the genuine Christian life is likely very ordinary. But it is an ordinariness permeated with God's character. And God is love. That makes all the difference.

Some days later I was again meditating on Lamentations 3:22-23. It says, "The LORD's lovingkindnesses indeed never cease, For His compassions never fail. They are new every morning, Great is Thy faithfulness." If you just read that by itself you might draw the conclusion that this is some kind of victory statement. But when we survey the context the reality is different.

Lamentations is Hebrew poetry and very highly structured. The poem is an acrostic. Verses 1-3 each begin with the first letter of the Hebrew alphabet, and that pattern occurs throughout until all twenty-two letters have been used in a total of sixty-six verses. In that formalistic plan the writer, probably Jeremiah, expresses his deep emotions in living through his experience of God judging the capital city of Jerusalem about 600 BC.

It was a terrible time, and verse 19 says: "Remember my affliction and my wandering, the wormwood and bitterness." And verse 26 adds: "It is good that he waits silently For the salvation of the LORD." Most of those who did not die in that suffering were taken to captivity in Babylon.

In the middle of the unspeakable horrors of that time Jeremiah wrote of the LORD's lovingkindnesses, His compassion, and His great faithfulness. How can that be? Would it not seem more likely that Jeremiah would join Job's wife in saying, "Let's curse God and die"? Yet Jeremiah experienced God as good and loving.

His experience resonated with me. God knows I would avoid any suffering possible, and yet in our suffering He showed Himself to be good and kind.

CHAPTER 13

STAGE FOUR—ACUTE REHAB AT NEW HOPE (PART 2)

After Two Weeks

Ruth was having up to four hours of therapy a day. After two weeks she had made tremendous progress. She was learning to walk with a walker. She began to learn how to negotiate steps again. Her left ankle began to get some movement; she could push down with that foot, but movement up was still impossible.

The therapists were practical, too. Ruth had a tendency to become tangled in the blankets in bed; she said they felt like ropes. So Diane had a session teaching her how to turn over in bed without getting tangled.

The recreational therapist took her to the cafeteria one day so she would have to deal with obstacles and people in public. She had to order for herself. One day she fried an egg. And of course she continued to play piano. She even played for other patients and accompanied hymn singing.

In occupational therapy she was able to do her laundry at New Hope. She had no difficulty with it beyond the fact that she was using unfamiliar equipment.

The speech therapist continued his challenges. One day he read scrambled sentences to Ruth, and she had to unscramble them. Then he would read little stories to her and ask her questions about them.

I was given freedom during this time to take Ruth for rides in the wheel chair. I could help her into it from her bed, and then we could cruise the halls. There were places to go where we could look out and see the city. We could visit other floors. I even began to take her for walks with the walker. I had to remind her to lift her left knee high.

New Hope has distances marked on the walls of the hallways so that you can tell how far someone has gone. In some of those early walks we went the length of a football field. It was impressive to be able to relate it that way.

At the end of two weeks she had reached the goals they had set for four to six weeks. This was amazing! So they adjusted their goals to help her even more.

We were hoping that her mental confusion would lessen. I wrote on the Care Page:

> We are hoping the brain soon finds a way to communicate with the left foot. We are also hoping that the mental confusion Ruth has clears. In practical matters she is totally clear; in matters of who was where when, not so much.

In practical matters her memory was excellent. Before I went home one weekend, I asked her for instructions on doing the laundry. She knew exactly where everything was that I needed, she remembered the proper sequence, and she told me how much detergent to use. That was helpful, because I did not usually do laundry. But with her instructions, I was successful.

When Ruth began to awaken, she was still planning for Christmas. She could not remember the Community Bible Church's Christmas program. John, our Sunday School superintendent, had videotaped the program and sent us a copy of it on CD. One evening during this time Ruth and I watched it together. As soon as it began, she said, "Now I remember." I was blessed to see that she knew everyone in the video and enjoyed seeing the program again. She had been much involved in its preparation.

Discharge Date

We began to think about a discharge date. The forms on the wall included an entry for discharge. Ruth asked once when it would be, and we did not know. One complication was that previously I had made plans to accompany Cody, the manager of operations at our local Christian radio station, KGLE (AM 590), to the National Religious Broadcasters convention in Nashville, TN. I served on the board of directors for Friends of Christian Radio which owns the station, and our church sponsors me in a one-minute program that airs five days a week. The convention would take place February 18-21.

I had first thought that since Ruth would be at New Hope for four to six weeks I would leave from Billings and return there and eventually take her home. But now it seemed possible that she could be discharged sooner. So I talked with Merle, the admissions coordinator, about the possibility of her remaining until after the convention, and he said, "Oh, no. We would never keep her here that long." (This may not be word for word the quotation, but that was the gist of what he said.) He explained that after a time the progress plateaus, and then the therapy is no longer cost effective.

Diane told me that Ruth was ahead of where they had thought she would be by now. I rejoiced in that, but we gave the credit to God. Whatever His purposes in all of this, He continued to orchestrate every step of the way.

So January 30 we were informed that Ruth would be discharged February 8. There was rejoicing as I shared the news with our children and others. But this changed the arrangements I would have to make for my trip to the NRB.

What would it be like to be back home? We didn't know exactly, but Jessica, the occupational therapist, told me that Ruth would be able to do most everything. But she should not be left alone. If she was cooking, for example, someone would need to make sure that afterward the burners and oven were turned off. So she would need some monitoring for safety purposes, but otherwise she could return to at least her domestic duties.

The therapists gave instructions for changes that had to be made in the bathroom so that Ruth could safely take care of herself there. Some men from the church installed the necessary equipment so it would be ready when we returned.

A Glitch

In order to eat supper with Ruth, I had to fill out an order which was then faxed to the cafeteria on another floor. When the food was delivered one evening to the Diner's Club, my tray did not arrive. We waited for some time and then began the process of trying to solve the problem. First the nurse on duty phoned the cafeteria to tell them of the problem, and no one answered the phone; she did leave a message. A little later I decided I would go to the cafeteria to investigate.

The cashier arranged a meeting with the retail manager of food service. He explained that rehab had failed to fax my order to the cafeteria. So he offered me either $10 or the meal I had ordered plus a voucher for a free meal. I chose the latter. So they rustled up a tray for me.

In the end I still didn't get my entire order: they gave me grapes instead of ice cream and milk instead of cranberry juice. Oh, well. The next time I ordered I asked if they could refrain from faxing the order so I might get another free meal. They responded that they better not because someone might catch on to this scam! We did have some fun with the staff there.

Another Glitch

Halfway through the stay at New Hope Ruth reported to me several mornings in a row that a certain doctor was daily accusing her of simply doing whatever her husband wanted. The arrangement had been for Ruth to receive sleeping pills if she needed them (she was taking no other medication at this time). Well, they had been giving them to her, and she consistently awakened at 3 AM. Thinking that perhaps that was when the pill lost its effectiveness, I suggested she try sleeping without the pills. She still had the option of requesting them.

So she tried without, and that was when this doctor made those accusations. I thought it was unfair of Ruth to have to put up with this. So I sought an opportunity to talk with the doctor about what seemed to me was a case of pushing her feminist ideas onto Ruth.

February 1 when I saw her near the nurse's station I simply asked her whether it was ethical for a physician to push a particular political view onto her patient. She naturally wondered what I had in mind. So I told her what Ruth had been reporting.

She responded that Ruth's mind wasn't very clear, so I should not take seriously what Ruth was saying. I answered her by saying that Ruth was actually quite clear and that in any case she understood relationships very well. Then the doctor responded by saying, "Well, I am her doctor." To which I replied that I had been her husband for over forty years.

After thanking each other for each other's contribution toward Ruth's health, we parted ways. The next morning she met Ruth in the Diner's Club when all the rehab patients were there eating and told her if she wanted a private conference she would come to her room. We don't really know why she said that. She then had some days off, and we never saw her again. She was the only doctor we really did not appreciate, since her feminist views appeared to affect her application of medicine. I concluded that she was perhaps a good doctor, but also a woman with an agenda.

After Three Weeks

The staff was really getting Ruth ready to go home. They had her practice getting into and out of a simulator car. One day I had to bring our car up to the entrance so she could practice getting in and out of it. Of course, that meant she had the rare opportunity of going outside.

One of her assignments in recreational therapy was to make pizza. She prepared ingredients over several days. Then the day finally came. I chuckled as I came in that morning: there she was, supervising the therapists. Kyle, the speech therapist, had his hands in the dough! They were inexperienced in making pizza, but Ruth was not. We had the privilege of eating it. It wasn't quite like her pizza at home, but it was excellent considering that she made it in a strange place without her own equipment and with not exactly the same ingredients.

At one point in making the pizza, Rosanna entered the room to find Ruth opening a second package of yeast. She questioned Ruth; it seemed she might not be thinking clearly. However, Ruth replied that in the limited time we had, the second package would help, and in any case it could not hurt. Ruth did know what she was doing, and it was a good decision. That particular day Ruth seemed to me to be more her old self than she had been previously; perhaps the activity of making pizza helped her to awaken further.

Probably the biggest challenge for her during this time was an outing of her choice. She selected going to a restaurant for breakfast. Her choice was Stella's, a place familiar to us and known for its pastries. It is also a place that is sympathetic to people with special needs; not all restaurants are.

Ruth would have to ask for a table in front. She would have to order. She would have to pay. And she would have to ask to use the restroom there with me assisting her. There are ways that restaurants can help a person in that situation.

So Ruth, Mary (a recreational therapist), and I went the last full day of her stay at New Hope. It was an enjoyable outing. Ruth used only the walker. Not only did she do well, but she had written a note to each of us, thanking us for our help. Here is mine; I still can hardly read it without tears.

> Dear Arlie,
>   I would never imagined spending days in a hospital. I could not have had someone better by my side than you!

Others have noticed, as they should all you've done and I have noticed, felt, and cherished your love. I can't believe all that you have coordinated, stays at several hospitals, interstate travel your schedule, helping Renessa, CBC needs and communication between family and friends.

You have stimulated me take advantage of opportunities to show love and good deeds. My understanding of what the Bible says and means has come because of your sermons and how you live your life. I pray Heb 6:10 for you, that God will not forget your ministering to me.

You have been kind and encouraging with my wobbly walking and my funky memory. And not reminding me of the bill that must be building.

I love you very much

Honey Bunch

Ruth

Transition

A couple days before discharge Renessa arrived from Central Asia with her two daughters, Alethia (3) and Maisie (1). She was able to be present for therapy training so that she could help Ruth at home. She was planning to stay about a month.

A friend, Brenda, volunteered to baby sit so that Renessa would be free during the day. Another friend, Heather, provided two car seats so that the girls could travel with us.

We were not sure how we would drive home the 220 miles from Billings because we would not all fit into our Hyundai Elantra. So Don and Deb loaned their Suburban again, and I was able to bring it back after being in Glendive for the final weekend.

The last full day was a day of testing and therapy geared to going home. The therapy would continue at home but without the therapists who had worked with Ruth there. We were grateful for them, but we were also glad that we could return home to establish some sort of normal life again.

One of the last maneuvers Diane taught Ruth was how to get down onto the floor and back up. It could be that Ruth would fall. She needed to know how to be somewhat independent and get up again.

One of the therapists remarked that it had been a pleasure to work with Ruth. She remarked that every day Ruth greeted them with a smile. It made their work more pleasant.

Ruth had not accomplished quite as much by the two-week mark in speech therapy, but we were very pleased that last day. I wrote the following in the Sequence:

> Kyle gave her a test he had given her at the beginning. She scored 26 out of 30 which he said was normal. Just three weeks ago she scored 12 which was moderate to severe. Thank you Lord! Praise God! We know the credit, the glory belongs to You!

Ruth wrote 'thank you' notes to the therapists before we left. We knew they were getting paid, but we appreciated them beyond the good service they had performed for her.

The trip home was uneventful, but it was a day of great rejoicing! It was a day of hope: hope that at one time had been uncertain and that was now fulfilled! Our house was still pre-Christmas. We would celebrate yet. And the first evening Ruth chose to wash the supper dishes. She had a chair behind her so she could sit down when she grew tired. It would be wonderful to be able to sleep in our bed together again!

We had asked if our church people would bring in several evening meals per week for maybe two weeks. They did, and it was a big help in becoming re-established at home. We had much catching up to do, new ways of learning to live, and company all at the same time.

As we returned home, I must tell you about one incident. Our schnauzer, Shadow, had stayed with dear friends who have three boxers. We wondered whether he would remember us after a fifty-one day absence. When I stopped to retrieve him, he came out with the boxers, and they all began to bark at this 'stranger.' But after several seconds his bark rose about an octave; he recognized me and welcomed me. We went home, and he fell right back into his old routine. And, as soon as it was possible, he jumped onto Ruth's lap, his favorite lap, to let her know that everything was good again.

This and That

Ruth was wondering near the end of her stay in Billings how we could thank everyone. I had wondered that often. We did often thank, but we had been served in ways we did not even know. I wrote one day in the Care Page:

> Ruth was wondering how we can ever thank everyone. That is a problem. Maybe we'll just have to say "Thank you" here, as inadequate as that is, and look to the Lord to bless them for it. He will surely not overlook their ministry to us when He assembles the rewards for the bema seat of Christ.

> "For God is not unjust so as to forget your work and the love which you have shown toward His name, in having ministered and in still ministering to the saints." (Hebrews 6:10)

One day one of the nurses came and asked where to find the Bible passage that lists the fruit of the Spirit. I was pleased as Ruth answered "Galatians 5:22-23." This nurse for a reason unknown to us was writing the fruit of the Spirit on the pillar in the Diner's Club where all the patients could see it. She had forgotten two of the nine.

One she had forgotten was 'longsuffering.' Another nurse didn't think longsuffering was such a good idea. Well, it sounds as though the Spirit causes you to suffer a long time. But I explained the meaning: it means that it takes a long time for you to get angry; you don't 'fly off the handle.' When she heard that, she said she needed it. So we talked about all of us needing that and that it is the Holy Spirit of God who provides it.

At meal time in the Diner's Club everyone ate together. Near the end of our stay, we remarked that there had been almost a complete turnover of people. We noticed one day a young girl with her head in a halo. There was a man with an amputated leg. There was a woman with an arm in a brace. There were some with significant stitched incisions on their heads. We enjoyed getting acquainted and hearing their stories.

Our children had lots of ideas about what should be changed and arranged when we would get home. These were especially those children who had seen Ruth in Denver. All of their ideas came out of love, but some of them were unnecessary. At one point I told them that Ruth was light years ahead of where she had been when they had seen her last, and she was! And really, in some ways we just wanted to get home where we could simplify and begin to live again without so many people being involved.

It was difficult for Ruth to think sometimes about what the costs must be. For quite a while we would not mention costs in her presence; we believed there would be a proper time for that later. I wrote in the Sequence near the end of our stay in Billings:

> Ruth has been moved to tears a couple
> times thinking about all the expense she
> 'has caused.' We have reassured her that
> I, the children, and lots of other people
> believe she is worth it. And we are speaking
> the truth. I have also told her that I know
> she would have done the same for me—she
> knows she would have.

CHAPTER 14

STAGE FIVE—AT HOME AGAIN

As I write this chapter, more than six months have passed since Ruth returned home. Some significant developments have transpired, and life has changed in certain ways. It is the same as before and yet different.

Ruth learned to use the wheelchair before leaving Billings. She never used it again. She used the walker for a few weeks, but then graduated to a cane. Before long she walked without the cane.

A few days after returning to Glendive she was evaluated for speech, physical, and occupational therapies. The speech therapist tested her cognitive abilities and said she did not need to return. That assessment was not a total surprise to us since her mind really was practically back to normal.

She did attend physical and occupational therapies two times a week for two months. We were impressed again at the excellence of her therapists; they evaluated her well and assigned the exercises that helped her recovery.

The changes needed in the bathroom had been made by men from the church so Ruth could safely use everything there. We had thought about furniture rearrangements that might be necessary, but in the end they were few. I moved her computer from the basement recreation room to the main-floor guest bedroom. We moved our kitchen/dining room table closer to one wall so there was enough room for the walker. And we removed the bathroom door because the walker was too wide for it. (Later a therapist moved the wheels on the walker from the outside of the legs to the inside, and then we could remount that door!)

Renessa and her girls were with us at home for about three and one-half weeks. They helped in a variety of ways, and in other ways they were a good distraction. They joined us in celebrating Christmas and my birthday even though the actual calendar dates were long past.

A couple months after we returned home, we went to visit the physician's assistant who was on duty in ER the night of

Ruth's injury. We just wanted to thank him for his attentive help that evening.

He said he was delighted to shake Ruth's hand. He related to us that on that December evening there had been nothing they could do for her. At that point he hoped that I had great support, because I was going to need it. Then he saw the group from our church and those several pastors standing outside the emergency room praying, and he knew that I had support.

He also said that doctors would still be shaking their heads at this case ten years from now. In his Sunday School class someone had asked how it could be that Ruth had been considered hopeless that night and yet now had returned home to live almost normally. His reply was that those decisions were not made on earth. He humbly stated to us that doctors are not in control; in fact, they are third or fourth down the line.

We were so glad we had gone back to talk with him. We were grateful for him, and he thought he had done nothing. But he had been faithful in doing his job.

Ruth was informed before leaving Denver that she should come back in six months. So June 25, a Monday, she had an appointment to meet with Dr. Bellon, who had done the coiling.

We arrived the Saturday before and ate supper at a Thai restaurant across the street from Swedish Medical Center. After eating I suggested we walk over to the hospital. It was all new to Ruth—as though she had never been there before. We went to seventh floor where she had recovered, and at least a half dozen nurses were present who had cared for her. Some of them recognized us almost immediately. They were delighted to see her, and she even received some hugs.

The angiogram Monday revealed some compaction of the coil. So they installed some additional coil and a stent. The procedure lasted over an hour, and Ruth needed to stay in critical care overnight.

Before any procedure the medical team gives a list of what can go wrong; the list included stroke and even death. When Ruth was unconscious and at death's door, it was easy to say "Go ahead." Now that she was relatively normal I had second thoughts. Of course I did finally say "Go ahead," but it seemed that now I was taking a calculated risk. I did realize that our doctors were doing their professional best and supporting all was the knowledge that we were still in the hands of God who had demonstrated His love to us abundantly.

When I came back the next morning, Ruth was dressed and ready to go. It was a vast improvement over the previous time.

Dr. Warner, the critical care physician, was very excited when she discovered that Ruth was playing piano again. She said that Dr. Bellon must be told. (He was.) So Ruth asked about her excitement. She said that the bleed had been on the part of the brain that relates to music. So Ruth asked, "Do you mean I could have lost that?" And she answered that Ruth could have lost all her musical ability. So Ruth has joined us all in being thankful to God for the return of her ability to play.

For a three-month period after that procedure she took a blood thinner. As a result she bruised easily. Also, the thinner blood caused any little cut to catch our attention, because the blood did not clot quickly. So care was in order.

Before we left Denver one of the doctors said that because of the blood thinner we should do no kayaking. I'm not sure why he chose that sport; we have never been involved in it. But I did ask about motorcycling. We didn't get a clear answer. The guideline was to avoid activities that are necessarily attended by danger. Maybe nothing bad would happen, but on the other hand virtually any activity in life can result in harm. So, again, caution was in order.

Ruth is back to doing just about everything she did before. About a month after returning home she returned to teaching piano. She had first thought she would proceed with the youngest students, but after rethinking she called her older students because they were preparing for music festivals. She was able to prepare them and encourage them through their competitions. She also had her annual spring recital.

As summer approached she called other students. Most of her students had transferred to other teachers, and she was careful not to try to get them back unless that was their choice. So she is currently teaching with a lighter load than she once had.

Ruth read online that an aneurysm patient will return home, recognize her kitchen as her kitchen, and at the same time feel as if everything is new. She did experience that. When she made pizza, an old and established practice for her, she would think, "Do I know how to do this?" When she used yeast she would think, "Do I know how to use this?" Instead of just using old tried and true recipes, she often has now gone online to find new recipes.

She approached her studio similarly. What was in all those music books on the shelves? She discovered what was in them by perusing them all and getting rid of some. It was a great refresher activity.

Ruth is back to driving mostly when someone else is with her. She has driven in town and out of town. Can she drive alone? Yes, and she has done some. She welcomes some coaching when changes need to be made. Our rule has been that the first time she does something, I need to be with her; maybe after that she can do it alone. She is ok with that.

She is again mowing our home lawn. She also mowed the church lawn in the past, but the church hired it done. It would have been too much for her now.

Her left ankle especially is still not as strong and flexible as the right one, and this does affect her balance and confidence. We do elastic band exercises almost every night to work on that. We have found that long walks are helpful. Before the injury happened she would often one day a week walk to Dawson Community College and back home. The round trip to the gate and back is 3.2 miles. I suggested one day that we make it a goal by June 2013. (Well, we began those walks and added about a block each time. By September 14, 2012, we made it!) Often the day after a long walk her ankle feels like it has made some progress. I should add that her consistent long distance walking is slower than before; it seems that the brain requires a bit more time to send messages to that left leg.

Her emotions are not as controlled as they were in the past. Crying comes more easily, and so does laughing. Crying can easily be stimulated by praying, by reading the Bible, by observing others in need, and by no reason at all. Laughing can easily be stimulated by me. She says I'm funny; I think sometimes she is funny. Sometimes she laughs and cries at the same time. But laughing is good, and we laugh together much more than previously.

Ruth is fully involved in the home, in church, and in society again. And I am thankful to God that she is still here beside me.

CHAPTER 15

THE OTHER SIDE
OF STAGE FIVE

One of the themes Ruth emphasized in raising our children is that they would learn to be kind. I have been amazed at the kindness of others to us, to me. Often it has been exhibited by people who know us, but it has also been demonstrated by complete strangers. And it surely is a blessing from God.

I was somewhat emotional in church yesterday, especially during the singing. The songs were wonderful, and I did sing heartily. I am overwhelmed again and again with God's love to us. It seems kind of unusual, when I consider it, that in this sort of time of suffering I am impressed with God's love. But I am, and I'm not going to try to analyze it. I just thank Him and praise Him.

I am usually on the end of ministering to others. To be on the other side of it is fascinating to contemplate. I seem to be hungry when I attend the church service. It is easy to tune in, to concentrate on the songs, on the Scripture, on the message. It feeds my soul. There is nothing superficial about it. Appetite is good.

from the Care Page

People often ask how we are doing. In general we are doing ok, at the same time life is different. It may seem curious, but it is really difficult to remember how life was before. This is our life now.

Someone along the way told me this would change us. My goal was to not allow this experience to define us by dominating every conversation and affecting every part of life from here on. Yet it stares us in the face every day.

Frequently in my sermon preparation I think of how this journey could provide an illustration, but I don't know how often I should make use of it. I don't think our congregation should have a steady diet of it. I make use of it far less than I could.

The whole experience has taken its toll. Perhaps we have aged throughout—someone noted that I had surely turned grayer! Some days we lack enthusiasm. Some days we are easily discouraged. But we do know that there is encouragement in the Lord, and we go to His word, the Bible, to receive it. The Lord often sends encouragement also through someone else when we need it.

Each of us is more sensitive to the whereabouts of the other person. If I'm not sure where Ruth is and if the house seems very quiet, I do sometimes check on her. And she sometimes tells me even after my absence of only a couple hours that she missed me.

I have severely restricted my piano tuning so that I am hardly ever away from home for an entire day. In the past I was even occasionally away overnight when I had enough work scheduled in a distant community.

Some years ago when my then elderly father stayed with us, we made plans for possible changes at various stages of growing older. Curiously, one of the changes was to cut back in the piano work about this time. I always wondered how that would happen, because I enjoyed the work and driving out of town to work farther away provided some pleasure. But with the sequence of events that became ours, the change was not difficult to effect.

Though we have always been together probably more than many other couples since my office is at home, we are doing more together than we were. In some respects we had each our own responsibilities and went our own way in them. Of course only she can do certain tasks, but I do help with some domestic duties more often, and we walk together more often. At the same time, it is good for her to do by herself what she can—it's all therapy!

Ruth has always enjoyed exercise, but now she has assigned exercises. I also exercise and lift weights, but now we tend to do them at the same time. That enables us to visit as we work out and to encourage each other. We also take therapeutic walks together.

People have called Ruth a "walking miracle." Some have asked whether God worked a miracle; others have assured us that He did. It may have been a miracle in the sense that what medical professionals expected at the beginning did not happen—there was a marked change in her condition between the time of being at the Glendive Medical Center and being at the Billings Clinic two hours later. There was a remarkable timing in the sequence of events and 'unscripted' details that were significant in the outcome. I, too, have stopped to consider the possibility of a miracle, but after looking at the evidence I have concluded that her recovery was not a miracle except colloquially speaking. So, though I disagree it was a miracle, I understand why some say it was.

When Jesus healed the paralyzed man who was let down through the roof in Luke 5, that man rose, took up his bed, and went home. Ruth could not do that when she left the hospital. When Peter and John at the Beautiful Gate in Acts 3 gave the man who had been lame from birth what they had, namely, the power and authority to heal him, he walked and leapt. Ruth still cannot jump, run, or begin to ride a bicycle.

Her recovery is amazing, but it may not have been a miracle by biblical definition. If Jesus had worked a miracle of the kind He worked in New Testament times, she would not have needed months of rehabilitation with lingering effects. That robs nothing from the good He has done, and whatever purposes He has in this will be realized through what she is now, not through what we might imagine a full recovery to be. Ruth often says that "God chose to give me life," and He did!

I wrote earlier that we appreciated the medical people who served us. We have the highest regard and appreciation for them. They appeared to do what was right and to do it with confidence, professionalism, expertise, and yet with a sense of humanness. For example, Dr. Bellon, the physician who did the coiling, told us after the return checkup to Denver, "We are thrilled with her progress!" And when I expressed our appreciation, he replied, "We do the best we can." For us "their best" was the perfect answer to Ruth's injury.

The financial side of all this took months to resolve. We do not have health insurance, but we are members of Samaritan Ministries, which is a medical cost-sharing network for Christians. Monthly each member is to send a share to an assigned person who has a medical need.

All of the medical procedures were costly, and the fact that four hospitals with different policies were involved made the process complicated. Mostly through the negotiations of our sons, the bills received significant discounts. And the members of Samaritan Ministries shared with us so the bills could be paid.

Close to a thousand members shared in our expenses. Along with the checks most of them sent cards with notes. Some of the members had passed through difficult experiences as well. It became a great blessing to read those, as we did over numerous special coffee times, and it further blessed us to realize that these people all over the country, people of like precious faith, joined us in giving and in prayer. The value of this blessing cannot be exaggerated.

Some wonder what the purpose is in all of this. I do not presume to know the complete answer. It may be that there are purposes that affect others, but I can only share what it may be for us. God's love has been made known to us in a focused way even though we are two insignificant people. We sense His love in that He specifically and directly cared for us and delivered us. He obviously loves us much as Romans 8 indicates. God's mercy has been expressed to me. You can read more about that in the last chapter. But His mercy and grace have become factors that are now impacting our decision making more than in the past. If He has been so gracious to us, how can we not be gracious to others?

The response of our children reflected back to us our investment in the biblical pattern for families outlined in Deuteronomy 6. We pursued the instruction of verses 5-7:

> "You shall love the LORD your God with all your heart and with all your soul and with all your might. And these words, which I am commanding you today, shall be on your heart; and you shall teach them diligently to your sons and shall talk of them when you sit in your house and when you walk by the way and when you lie down and when you rise up."

Later in that same chapter the parents are to be ready to answer the faith questions the children will ask. Other passages, many in Proverbs and some in the epistles, rounded out the plan we pursued in rearing our children. Rather than giving attention to certain formalities that are well-known, e.g., family devotions, children's prayers, and children's giving, we endeavored to make the discussion of God's word a family activity throughout the experiences of life. Now we look back and are not disappointed with the choices we made.

Throughout the crisis, our children came to be physically with us, they gave us ordinary stuff that made the duration of the crisis easier, they participated in the therapy, they supplied advice that we requested, they managed the finances involved, and best of all they fellowshipped with us in conversations concerning the things of God. At this time, all we had poured into their lives as they grew up in our home came back to bless us. I marveled again and again at the richness of the love we shared.

In the pastorate it is easy to be impacted negatively by the congregation. I know that personally, and I hear it from other pastors as well. But through this journey we have seen the Body of Christ, as represented by our local church and by the larger Christian community, acting like Christ, the Head, in caring, providing, and bearing the load. Our hope is that in the days we have left we will not forget or suppress what we have been privileged to learn through God's discipline.

To communicate via telephone, email, snail mail, Care Page, etc. may seem like a small gesture to those on the outside. But to me it was a breath of life. I longed for communication, and this was one way the Body of Christ encouraged me. Some also gave gifts such as a Starbucks card or cash or a meal or transportation, and every gift regardless of size was helpful. Nothing was received that was not somehow significant and strengthening.

There are purposes which directly and definitely involve Ruth. King Hezekiah of Judah, in Isaiah 38, had been informed that he would die young. He complained to the LORD, not because he misunderstood death and the hereafter but because he (like the psalmist in Psalm 6:5; 30:9; 88:12) understood that when a believer dies prematurely there is one less person on earth to give the testimony of praise to God and to pass on the knowledge of God to the next generation. These purposes are significant. Ruth continues to fulfill these.

I cannot omit the purpose she has regarding me—I would be negligent if I did. She has been returned to me to walk beside me the rest of this life as my complement. This is huge for me!

Finally, throughout this journey I was surprisingly brought back again and again to the central blessing of having a relationship with the Lord Jesus Christ. That mattered most, and it continues to be so. We are bothered about many life-issues, but belonging to Him is primary and most comforting.

I am reminded of the account recorded in Luke 10. Jesus had sent out the seventy disciples in pairs to prepare people for His visits to follow. After their mission was complete, they returned with great rejoicing. He had given them authority to perform miracles along with their message, and they had. They had even been able to cast out demons!

Naturally they were excited about all this. But Jesus told them not to rejoice in those spectacular miracles. He said in verse 20, "Nevertheless do not rejoice in this, that the spirits are subject to you, but rejoice that your names are recorded in heaven." There was a multitude of concerns over Ruth's trauma and subsequent recovery, but through it all that fact that her name and mine are recorded in heaven outweighed all.

> "Thus says the LORD, 'Let not a wise man boast of his wisdom, and let not the mighty man boast of his might, let not a rich man boast of his riches; but let him who boasts boast of this, that he understands and knows Me, that I am the LORD who exercises lovingkindness, justice, and righteousness on earth; for I delight in these things,' declares the LORD" (Jeremiah 9:23-24).

CHAPTER 16

MERCY FOR ME

No doubt you've been wondering about that title for the book. It doesn't sound as though it is about Ruth. And in a way it's not. She is the central figure, but this is the story of how I received mercy. I have received abundant mercy.

It would have been to Ruth's advantage to have died. She had lived a full life, and to die would mean to be ushered into the presence of the Lord forever and to be gone from the trials of life in the land of the dying. She had trusted the Lord Jesus Christ as the sacrifice for her sins, and her ultimate home is heaven. There was no negative in that for her. But that result for me, though I knew it could have been God's will—and in that case His grace would have been somehow adequate—seemed to be devastating. I did not want to take any blessing away from her, but for myself I could not see how I could continue.

145

My experience identifies with the Apostle Paul's recorded in Philippians 2:27. Epaphroditus had been sick and was now well. This is what Paul wrote: "For indeed he was sick to the point of death, but God had mercy on him, and not on him only but also on me, lest I should have sorrow upon sorrow."

Almost from the start I could not escape the realization that I was the recipient of great mercy from God, which manifested itself in various ways. A simple understanding of mercy is that it is misery removed. It is in some sense the other side of grace or undeserved favor. I experienced again and again the removal of misery that could well have been my lot. And I write that without any sense of glibness. Let me share three ways in which I received mercy.

The first way I received mercy was in the removal of my loss. When I found Ruth crumpled on the floor, I knew that her departure from this life was only a breath away. That uncertainty continued for over a week. (Of course, in a sense that uncertainty is always here, but then it was forefront.) When the evidence began to indicate that she would live, I was ecstatic! I had been given great mercy! Ruth would live, and for now I would not have to endure that extreme misery of learning to live without her.

The second way I received mercy was in Ruth regaining functions she had lost. Even when we knew she would live, medically speaking there was no way the professionals could predict the level of her recovery. Obviously I desired her return to normal or at least some measure of it. I was grateful for her life, and I thought I could be satisfied with that. But function began to return.

We look back on those early days. It is very important to be able to swallow (you might want to stop and think about that for a while) and to talk—to communicate verbally. She was given back those abilities. Wow!

It is important to be able to sit up. I had never considered that you could lose the strength to do that. She looked much better sitting up and seemed to take more interest in what was around her once she had that strength.

Therapists worked with her to regain muscle tone in hands, arms, legs, and feet. They were helping her prepare to use her hands and feet. But along the way she was given the opportunity to sit at the piano. God gave back her ability to play. Tremendous! So much of her life revolved around piano, and I could imagine her playing again at home and myself hearing her in the background as I worked in the office. That was a gift about which we had wondered.

Along with these therapies there were other exercises including efforts to stimulate thinking and reasoning. As each function reappeared, I realized anew the mercies of God. There were no guarantees that Ruth would function again on this level, and each advance promised her a bit more independence, a bit more of normal life even for me.

The third way I received mercy was in the reversal of loss that other similar patients have not experienced. This is a difficult area for me. We know of others with similar injury who have not had the recovery Ruth has. Why? I have no answer that can put myself or anyone else at ease.

I do know this: Ruth's recovery has nothing to do with how deserving we are. This is all about God's goodness, not ours. We experienced an extreme trauma for seven weeks away from home and after that a continuing long-term recovery at home. Others have experienced death or maybe life with very little recovery. They go on day after day with no visible hope of better days ahead, at least not here on earth. How do they do it?

But the Lord has a different journey for each of us. I expect that from the perspective of heaven none of us will fault the Lord for the way He has assigned us. He uses our experiences in a variety of ways of His own choosing, and we may never know exactly what those are. I wish I could clarify more than that, and this may sound like a platitude, but it is not so intended.

My heart goes out to others in their sufferings, and I pray for them to also know God's goodness and love. Why I have experienced certain mercies they have not I cannot explain.

I can't be sure what the lessons are. If it can be explained, it must be our Sovereign Creator God who does it. And He does love each of us more than we can imagine, more than we even love ourselves. This is apparent when we take a look at the Lord Jesus Christ.

Do you understand the title now? The Lord did not give Ruth back for her own good; she has much unexpected and in a sense unwelcome work trying to gain back her former level of strength, balance, and flexibility. He gave her back for my sake. Her return is mercy for me. She is a daily reminder to me of God's mercy. And I praise Him!

I deeply appreciate the doctors, nurses, and other medical personnel who helped us expertly during this extreme time. Yet it was God who gave life and the opportunity for recovery, and it was God the Creator who gave medical scientists the understanding necessary to develop the means used today to save and restore life. Though the context is a bit different, allow me to paraphrase Psalm 20:7 in a way valid to our experience: "Some trust in doctors and nurses and some in technology; but we will boast in the name of the LORD our God."

The book of Lamentations was presumably written by Jeremiah during the time of the fall of Jerusalem at the hands of the Chaldeans almost 600 years B.C. In what was a terrible time of suffering he wrote:

The LORD's lovingkindnesses indeed never cease, For His compassions never fail. They are new every morning; Great is Thy faithfulness. "The LORD is my portion," says my soul, "Therefore I have hope in Him" The LORD is good to those who wait for Him, To the person who seeks Him. It is good that he waits silently For the salvation of the LORD . (Lamentations 3:22-26)

I must say that I hope you know the mercies of God. No one will be in heaven without experiencing at least some of His mercy. Titus 3:4-7 says,

But when the kindness of God our Savior and His love for mankind appeared, He saved us, not on the basis of deeds which we have done in righteousness, but according to His mercy, by the washing of regeneration and renewing by the Holy Spirit, whom He poured out upon us richly through Jesus Christ our Savior, that being justified by His grace we might be made heirs according to the hope of eternal life.

The greatest misery is to exist throughout life on earth apart from God and then to transition at death to eternal separation from God. You might notice that throughout the above quotation there is no mention of what you need to do to gain eternal life. God has done it all in Jesus Christ our Savior. He asks you to believe, to depend on Him and what He has done. Ruth and I rejoice today that the misery of eternal separation from God is not our future. It doesn't have to be yours, either.

CPSIA information can be obtained at www.ICGtesting.com
Printed in the USA
BVOW08s0408300114

343420BV00001B/1/P

9 781490 822105